THE KINGFISHER
YOUNG PEOPLE'S BOOK OF
SPACE

THE KINGFISHER
YOUNG PEOPLE'S BOOK OF
SPACE

MARTIN REDFERN

NEW YORK

Author Martin Redfern
Consultant Dr. Paul Murdin, OBE
Project Editor Clive Wilson
U.S. Editors Aimee Johnson, Jenny Siklós
Design Traffika Publishing Limited
Art Editor Susan Aldworth
DTP Operator Primrose Burton
Picture Researcher Veneta Bullen
Researchers Adam Hibbert, Laura Sheppard
Production Susan Wilmot, Richard Waterhouse
Indexer Hilary Bird

Larousse Kingfisher Chambers Inc.
95 Madison Avenue
New York, New York 10016

First published in 1998
2 4 6 8 10 9 7 5 3 1

LIBRARY OF CONGRESS CATALOGING-IN-PUBLICATION DATA
Redfern, Martin.
The Kingfisher young people's book of space / Martin Redfern.—
1st ed.
p. cm.
Includes index.
Summary: Examines our exploration of outer space and discusses the
solar system, stars, galaxies, and the universe in general.
1. Outer space—Juvenile literature. 2. Outer space—Exploration—
Juvenile literature. 3. Planets—Exploration—Juvenile literature.
(1. Outer space. 2. Astronomy.) I. Title.
QB500.22.R4   1998
520—dc21   97-51122   CIP AC

ISBN 0-7534-5136-0

Color separations by Newsele
Printed in Singapore

CONTENTS

A Place in the Cosmos

Our ancestors once believed that the Earth must be the center of the Universe. Every morning they watched the Sun rise in the east and move across the sky. At night, the Moon, stars, and planets filled the darkness, and all appeared to revolve around the Earth. For almost a thousand years, the Church encouraged this view because it placed humans, God's special creation, at the center. By the 1500s, some astronomers began to argue that the Earth went around the Sun and, in the end, their evidence was overwhelming. Since then we have discovered that the Universe has no real center. We inhabit one of nine planets orbiting a medium-sized star in a galaxy containing billions of other stars. This galaxy itself is just one among billions of other galaxies. The search for our place in the Universe must be played out on an altogether bigger stage than ever imagined by our ancestors. And that search is the story of this book.

△ *Great stone calendars such as Stonehenge, built over 4,000 years ago, helped people keep track of the Sun's daily and yearly movements.*

△ *Over 1,800 years ago, Ptolemy set out the Greek scholars' view of an Earth-centered Universe. This Christian version was painted in 1493.*

△ *The Copernican model of the Universe has the Sun at its center. Copernicus first published his ideas in 1543.*

The view from Greece

In 270 B.C., a Greek philosopher called Anaxagoras suggested that the Earth went around the Sun. His ideas seemed so ridiculous to the people of Athens that he was thrown out of the city! Aristotle's theory, developed by Ptolemy in about A.D. 120, put the Earth at the center of the Universe with the planets revolving around it in simple circles.

Heavenly revolutions

Nicolaus Copernicus and Galileo Galilei suggested that calculations explaining the motions of planets only made sense if the Earth went around the Sun. Aristotle's model of a Sun-centered Universe was finally overturned in 1610 when Galileo, using his newly invented telescope, discovered that Jupiter had moons orbiting it.

True scale of the Universe

Our galaxy *(right)*, lies in a tiny corner of the Universe. The Sun, around which we orbit at an average distance of 93 million miles (150 million km), is only a dot in one of the galaxy's spiral arms. Light takes 100,000 years to reach the Earth from the other side of the galaxy and ten billion years from the farthest galaxies.

▽ *Albert Einstein provided the framework for our modern understanding of the Universe. In 1915, he proved that space and time cannot be clearly separated, and space itself is curved.*

△ *Edwin Hubble was the first person to prove that there are galaxies other than our own. In the late 1920s, he showed that the galaxies are rushing apart from each other and that the Universe is expanding.*

Looking Up

△ *Galileo's detailed sketches of the Moon were made using the telescope he constructed in 1609.*

In 1609, news reached Italy that a Dutch instrumentmaker had used two curved pieces of glass in a tube to magnify a distant object. The first lens focused the object into an image, and the second magnified it. The Italian astronomer Galileo realized that this "telescope" could be used to observe the sky, and the heavens became open to serious astronomical study. With this new scientific instrument, Galileo revealed four moons orbiting Jupiter, evidence for the idea that the planets might in turn orbit the Sun. The first telescopes used lenses. Reflecting telescopes, invented in the 1660s, have a concave mirror instead of a lens to focus and catch starlight. The mirror needs to be curved on only one side, so it can be made bigger and can detect fainter objects in greater detail.

▽ *William Herschel's telescope, completed in 1789, was used to study and calculate the distribution of thousands of stars throughout space.*

▷ The 100-inch Hooker Telescope *on Mount Wilson, California, remained the biggest and most powerful telescope in the world until 1948.*

◁ *The* Very Large Array *is a series of 27 radio telescopes in the New Mexico desert. Together they have the resolution of an instrument 17 miles (27 km) across, and provide detailed maps of distant galaxies.*

◁ *The 14-foot (4.2-m) William Herschel Telescope is built on a high, dry mountain peak on La Palma in the Canary Islands. The lines in the sky are the trails of stars.*

Mirror power

A reflecting telescope's power depends on the size of its mirror. The latest generation of telescopes have mirrors over 26 feet (8 m) in diameter. Computers keep the mirrors in alignment. When it is completed in 2002, the *Very Large Telescope* in Chile will have the power to spot a firefly 6,214 miles (10,000 km) away.

High and dry

Even on a clear night, the Earth is not a perfect place to put a telescope. Water vapor and turbulence in the atmosphere blur the images and make the stars seem to dance around. In order to avoid this, optical telescopes are usually built on mountains. But even there, the window of the Universe is not fully open—visible light is just one part of a whole spectrum of different wavelengths.

Radio waves

Besides light, only radio waves can penetrate the Earth's atmosphere. Radio waves are longer than light waves, so radio telescope mirrors do not have to be so finely polished. Today, individual radio telescopes on different continents can be linked by computer to give the equivalent of a single dish thousands of miles wide.

◁ *The 100-inch* Hooker Telescope's *glass mirror (located at the other end of the tube) was cast at a French wine bottle factory. The "100-inch" part of its name refers to the diameter of the telescope's mirror.*

▽ *Light is only one octave on the great keyboard of the electromagnetic spectrum. Only visible light and part of the radio spectrum penetrate far through the Earth's atmosphere.*

MICROWAVE	VISIBLE LIGHT	X RAY
RADIO	INFRARED	ULTRAVIOLET	GAMMA RAY

△ *High, dry mountain peaks provide the best location for observing the sky. This radio telescope (left) and optical telescope (right) are found at Cerro La Silla in the Andes Mountains of Chile.*

△ *The* Hubble Space Telescope, *launched from the space shuttle in 1990, has been a phenomenal success. Although its 8-foot (2.4-m) curved mirror was polished originally to the wrong shape, this was corrected in 1993. The* Hubble Space Telescope *can also "see" in the ultraviolet and infrared wavelengths.*

Looking Out

▽ *The* Infrared Space Observatory *detected heated radiation with a curved mirror. Liquid helium kept the sensors cool.*

△ *Images from the* Hubble Space Telescope, *such as this one of a dying star, are radioed back to Earth.*

A journey just a few miles up above the atmosphere opens up a whole new window to the Universe. There is no reflected glare of city lights to dazzle an observer, and there is nothing to blur the stars or make them twinkle. As a result, it is possible to see objects in far greater detail than from the ground. The *Hubble Space Telescope* is the first big optical telescope to be put into orbit. It has allowed astronomers to peer into the hearts of galaxies and out to the farthest reaches of the Universe. As well as visible light, there is also a full rainbow of radiation to explore, from microwaves and infrared, to ultraviolet, x rays, and gamma rays. The only drawback is that you have to launch your telescope into space!

△ *Launched from the space shuttle* Atlantis, *the* Compton Gamma Ray Observatory *is named after Arthur Holly Compton, an American scientist who pioneered the study of gamma rays.*

Heat detection

Infrared, or heat radiation, comes from warm objects that are not as hot as the stars we see. These include planets and comets, regions where new stars are forming, and distant galaxies ablaze with young stars. Although telescopes located on high mountains can see some infrared radiation, the first comprehensive study came with the *Infrared Astronomy Satellite (IRAS)* in 1983. In 1995, Europe's *Infrared Space Observatory (ISO)* was launched to look in even greater detail.

Gamma rays

Gamma rays are released by the most energetic processes in the Universe. These processes include matter falling into a black hole, matter and antimatter annihilating each other, and explosions in the cores of galaxies. Launched in 1991, the *Compton Gamma Ray Observatory* is an orbiting laboratory that has detected sudden bursts of gamma rays coming from every direction.

▷ Exosat *was designed to study x-ray sources. Between 1983 and 1986, it made and sent back reports of over 2,000 observations.*

Ultraviolet

Ultraviolet light comes from hot gas and stars. It carries the fingerprints of the atoms that emitted it and the gas clouds through which it has traveled. The *International Ultraviolet Explorer (IUE)* is one of the most successful astronomy satellites to date. Launched in 1978 with a planned life of three years, *IUE* focused the light with a 1.6-foot (0.5-m) mirror and, instead of taking a picture, spread the light out into the spectrum of wavelengths, revealing these atomic fingerprints. It was finally switched off in 1997 after nearly 19 years in service.

△ *The* International Ultraviolet Explorer *was the only ultraviolet observatory in space until the launch of the* Hubble Space Telescope *in 1990.*

Rise of the Rocket

Gravity keeps us earthbound. To escape its pull and leave our planet far behind, we need to travel at an incredible 7 miles (11 km) per second (about 24,900 miles [40,000 km] per hour). To reach such speeds calls for the power of a rocket. The first rockets were more like fireworks and followed China's invention of gunpowder in the 1000s. They used rocket-propelled flaming arrows, launched from a basket, against their enemies (*see picture above left*). Warfare continued to be the driving force in developing rocketry. During World War II, the V2 rockets of Nazi Germany terrorized British cities. Captured V2s were sent to the United States, and their successors, the intercontinental ballistic missiles, helped to launch the space age.

△ *Robert Goddard designed the first successful liquid-fuel rocket. Its maiden flight in March 1926 lasted 2.5 seconds.*

△ *After World War II, captured German V2 rockets, together with their inventor Wernher von Braun, played a key role in the U.S. space program.*

The pioneers

After the end of World War II, the pace of rocket research accelerated, with Wernher von Braun in the United States and Sergei Korolev in Russia leading the way. A race soon developed between the two superpowers—if a rocket could send a payload into Earth orbit, it could also deliver a bomb to the other side of the world.

Winners and losers

On October 4, 1957, the Soviet Union demonstrated they had the edge when they put *Sputnik 1*, a 23-inch (58-cm) aluminum sphere with a radio transmitter, into orbit. Meanwhile, the U.S. Navy *Vanguard* rocket blew up on the launchpad. Wernher von Braun was called in with his army team and on January 31, 1958, his *Jupiter-C* rocket put *Explorer 1*, the U.S.'s first satellite, into orbit.

◁ *The mighty* Saturn V *rocket lifts off from Cape Canaveral, Florida, on July 16, 1969 to put the first men on the Moon.*

◁ *Rockets often have several stages, each carrying its own oxygen with which to burn the fuel. The first stage of* Saturn V *had five great engines, burning 15 tons of kerosene and liquid oxygen every second. It produced a thrust of 3,500 tons and lasted for less than three minutes before falling back to Earth.*

◁ *Cosmonaut Yuri Gagarin was the first person to orbit our planet, on April 12, 1961.*

△ *On November 3, 1957, the Russian dog Laika became the first living creature to orbit the Earth. The craft, Sputnik 2, was not designed to return, and, after seven days, Laika was injected with poison.*

△ *A single motor, using liquid hydrogen, fired for two minutes to place the astronauts in Earth orbit; then again to set them on course for the Moon.*

▷ *Amateur rockets are becoming increasingly sophisticated and successful. With commercial sponsorship, amateurs try to reach space and launch small satellites.*

Spacemen

The first man in space followed shortly after the first satellite. Again, Russia won the race, launching Yuri Gagarin into a single Earth orbit on April 12, 1961. Three weeks later, Alan Shepard became the first American to be blasted into space, though not into orbit, landing 15 minutes later in the Atlantic. Finally, on February 20, 1962, the American John Glenn made three Earth orbits.

△ *Two seconds after the first stage broke away, the five rocket motors on the second stage fired, burning liquid hydrogen and liquid oxygen. This stage lasted for six minutes, during which time the escape tower (for use in a launchpad emergency) was jettisoned.*

Popular destination

Since the late 1950s, thousands of rockets have been launched and hundreds of people have visited space. But it has never become routine. The dangers are such that each mission involves thousands of people on the ground, checking and rechecking the complex systems of spaceflight.

| V2 | ATLAS | SOYUZ A2 | ARIANE | TITAN IIIE | SPACE SHUTTLE | SATURN V |

△ *At 360 feet (110 m) high, Saturn V towers over other rockets. These include the German V2, first used in 1944, and Atlas and Soyuz, which took astronauts into space. The Titan and Ariane launch satellites.*

Race to the Moon

As soon as rockets could break away from the Earth's gravity, the next goal became the Moon. It was a whole new world waiting to be explored—and claimed! The Russians again took the lead, landing the first craft on the Moon and photographing the dark, or far, side in 1959. Meanwhile, the United States launched 11 unmanned Moon missions, without one completing its objective. Then, on May 25, 1961, President Kennedy committed the country to putting a person on the Moon by 1970. The Apollo program began, and on July 21, 1969, *Apollo 11* landed the first astronauts on the Moon.

△ *From its Earth orbit, the final stage of the* Saturn V *rocket boosts the Command and Service Module (CSM) on its 250,000-mile (400,000-km) journey to the Moon. The CSM stays in orbit around the Moon while the lunar lander visits the surface. The lander rejoins the CSM for the journey home.*

▷ *Their mission completed, the lunar lander blasts off from the Moon, leaving the bottom half of the lander and a remote camera behind.*

△▷ *One astronaut stays orbiting the Moon in the CSM while the other two enter the lunar lander. The lander makes a vertical descent to the surface, using its single rocket to slow down the craft.*

UNITED STATES

△ *James Irwin salutes the U.S. flag in front of Apollo 15's lander, after returning with a collection of rocks on the lunar rover (right).*

▷ *Once the astronauts have rejoined the CSM, their lander ascent stage is jettisoned. It crashes back to the Moon's surface, sending shock waves to sensors already in place. These provide information about the structure of the Moon. The rocket on the CSM fires to return to Earth. Finally, the rocket is jettisoned and all that returns to Earth is the command module.*

Failure rate

From 1959 to 1976, there were 48 Russian and 31 American unmanned Moon missions. Of these, about half failed, but the pressure to get to the Moon was great, and both sides kept on trying. Reliability improved, but there were casualties: three U.S. astronauts died in the *Apollo 1* when fire broke out on the launchpad, and four Russian cosmonauts died returning from the *Salyut* space station.

△ *Parachutes slow the command module before splashdown into the sea. Airbags inflate to keep it upright as the astronauts disembark.*

A change of direction

To land people on the Moon and return them to Earth required a very powerful and reliable rocket. While the U.S. *Saturn V* fitted the bill, the Russian *N1* rocket suffered four failures. In 1974, Russia canceled its program and concentrated on establishing a permanent presence above the Earth with its space stations.

Houston, we have a problem

On April 13, 1970, *Apollo 13* was 56 hours into its flight when commander Jack Swigert reported, "We have a problem." An oxygen tank had exploded, and the astronauts had to conserve power, air, and water for four tense days before they could return to Earth.

LUNA 2   **LUNA 16**   **SURVEYOR**   **LUNOKHOD 1**   **APOLLO**

△ *In 1959, Russia's* Luna 2 *was the first space probe on the Moon. In 1970, the unmanned* Luna 16 *brought back Moon rocks. Five U.S. Surveyor craft landed in the 1960s. Russia's Lunokhod 1 traveled 6.5 miles (10.5 km) on the surface. Six Apollo spacecraft landed on the Moon.*

△ *As the command module meets the Earth's atmosphere, friction makes it glow red-hot.*

15

The Space Shuttle

After Apollo, the United States set out to create a cheaper alternative to maintain its presence in space. The space program wanted a craft that could go into orbit and return to the Earth again and again. The space shuttle was designed to do this, but it was not a simple task. A single-stage craft could not carry enough fuel to reach orbit. Instead, two solid-fuel rocket boosters and a giant, external fuel tank filled with liquid oxygen and hydrogen, power the shuttle almost into orbit. The shuttle orbiter is covered with 32,000 heat-resistant tiles, each shaped and attached by hand, which protect it on reentry into the atmosphere. *Columbia*, the first operational orbiter, made its maiden flight in April 1981.

Life in orbit

Life aboard a space shuttle is much more comfortable than that inside the cramped quarters of the Apollo modules. There is a wash room and bunk beds. The food is better, and there is plenty to do, with fantastic views of the Earth through the windows. After takeoff, the crew (of up to eight people) wears comfortable clothes. There are racks of experiments in the living quarters. In the cargo bay, satellites can be carried for launch, or retrieved for repair. Astronauts put on space suits and go out through an air lock to work outside the orbiter.

△ *Using a Manned Maneuvering Unit (MMU) like a sort of jet-propelled armchair, an astronaut can fly freely from the shuttle's cargo bay. The MMU is used to help retrieve faulty satellites, take photographs, or just to admire the view.*

▽ *A space shuttle blasts off from the Kennedy Space Center in Florida. The brilliant jet from the two solid-fuel rocket boosters (one of which is in the foreground) provides five times more thrust than the shuttle's three main engines (on the right).*

△ *Once in space, the shuttle orbiter can open its 60-foot (18-m)-long cargo-bay doors to deploy satellites, perform experiments, or point instruments at the Earth or into space.*

△ *At blastoff, the shuttle's main engines (using fuel from the external tank) and rocket boosters provide thrust equivalent to 140 jumbo jets. Two minutes later the boosters break away. Then the external tank falls away and it is MECO (Main Engine Cut-Off). After the mission is complete, the main engines slow the orbiter and it begins to fall, glowing red from friction, on reentry. It lands like a glider on a runway.*

◁ *Attempts to design a fully reusable spaceplane are now underway. Unlike the shuttle, spaceplanes will be able to take off as well as land on runways like conventional airplanes.*

Challenger disaster

No one wants a space mission to fail, but when there are people on board, safety is the most important issue. Launches are often delayed or called off at the last moment because of a slight change in the weather, a minor computer glitch, or a faulty sensor. On January 28, 1986, however, one fault proved fatal. A frosty night before the launch of shuttle *Challenger* caused the rubber "O" rings sealing the sections of its rocket boosters to become brittle. After takeoff, a flame from the rockets broke through a seal, sending a jet of fire onto the huge external fuel tank. Little more than a minute into the flight, the tank exploded and the seven astronauts were killed.

Satellite triumphs

After the *Challenger* disaster, shuttle missions were suspended for two and a half years. Since then, among the shuttle's biggest triumphs have been the refurbishment and repair of satellites. For example, after its launch in 1990, the *Hubble Space Telescope* was found to be faulty. In 1993, shuttle astronauts retrieved the telescope and repaired it in space.

▽ *One of the two solid-fuel rocket boosters veers away from the exploding wreckage of the* Challenger *shuttle just 73 seconds after liftoff.*

Unmanned competition

Although the shuttle is the most versatile manned spacecraft, the unmanned satellite launch market is very competitive. The U.S.'s leading competitor is the European Ariane rocket, with over 100 successful launches. Russia, China, Japan, and India also have rocket programs.

△ *The Soviet space shuttle* Buran *was much like the U.S. shuttle but had no engines itself, rising on the Energia rocket. It flew in space only once, in 1988, on an unmanned test.*

△ *The* Ariane 5 *rocket sits on its launchpad in French Guiana in June 1996. The first flight was a disaster (a computer fault caused it to veer off course), but the second succeeded. Unlike its rivals,* Ariane 5 *can launch up to four satellites at once.*

▷ *The* International Space Station *as it may look by 2003. Largely U.S.-built and serviced by the space shuttle, it will also carry modules from Russia, Europe, and Japan.*

△ *Spacelab is a pressurized module that flies in the cargo bay of the space shuttle. On this mission, in 1993, there were around 90 experiments, including ones on the effects of weightlessness on astronauts.*

▽ *Astronauts train underwater (inset) to simulate the effects of weightlessness in space and to practice repairing satellites. In space itself, an astronaut uses the shuttle's robot arm like a cherrypicker to control his or her movements above the open cargo bay.*

Living in Space

On May 27, 1973, the space station *Skylab* was launched. Made of modified *Saturn V* and Apollo units, it offered the first long-stay, orbiting laboratory for microgravity research and studying the Sun and the Earth. It also provided an opportunity to practice space repairs when the crew had to replace damaged shielding. Its last crew set a space endurance record when they spent 84 days living in *Skylab*. In 1977, the Russians launched *Salyut 6*, the first space station to have two air locks, allowing one crew to arrive before the other departed. This was replaced in 1982 by *Salyut 7* and then, in 1986, by *Mir*, in which the endurance record has been broken over and over again.

Working in space

In space, some of the most difficult tasks are Extra-Vehicular Activities (EVAs). A space suit must be worn as protection from the vacuum, radiation, and temperature extremes. Large objects, though weightless, still have mass and, once in motion, can wreak havoc. Even turning a screwdriver can cause problems. Unless an astronaut is well anchored, the screw stays in place while the astronaut rotates!

△ *In July 1995, the U.S. shuttle* Atlantis *docked with* Mir *and both crews posed for cameras. It was the start of a collaboration that provided much-needed cash for Russia's space program and hardware for the U.S.*

△ *The meals served on board the space shuttle are a great improvement on the dried and concentrated capsules given to Apollo astronauts.*

◁ *This unisex toilet is designed for the* International Space Station. *It comes with foot and thigh restraints. Air flow removes the waste, which is then dried and compressed.*

Space stations of the future

The *International Space Station* is due for launch in the late 1990s. It is a laboratory for microgravity research and provides a testing-ground for future plans. Space stations could serve as assembly points for interplanetary craft and manned missions to Mars. They could be used as astronomical observatories or factories for manufacturing new materials. A rotating space station with artificial gravity might even one day become a hotel for tourists.

◁ *Huge arrays of solar cells, assembled in space, provide the electrical power for the space station.*

Enduring *Mir*

The core module of the Russian space station *Mir* was launched in 1986 with a planned life of five years. Ten years later, surrounded by add-on modules, it started to show signs of aging. First, waste water pumps and air conditioning malfunctioned. The oxygen generators failed next, followed by a potentially serious fire which was caused by an oxygen-releasing candle. Then, in June 1997, an unmanned supply craft crashed into one of *Mir*'s modules, cutting forty percent of the power. Only Russian determination and U.S. money kept *Mir* going.

◁ *This close-up of* Mir, *taken from the space shuttle in August 1997, shows damage to a solar array* (right) *and a thermal radiator* (left). *The damage was caused by an unmanned* Progress *supply craft that crashed into* Mir's Specktr *module two months earlier.*

◁ *The Russian space station* Mir *was launched in 1986. Since then, several new modules have been added, increasing its mass from 21 tons to over 100 tons. Astronauts live and work in the largest module, which is 43 feet (13 m) long. The other modules are used for experiments and storing equipment. Handrails on* Mir's *exterior aid astronauts as they work outside.*

Using Space

Rocket launches are very expensive and not always reliable, yet governments and businesses are lining up for slots on board launch craft. Space is potentially so useful that it is well worth the risk and expense. Some satellites look at the Earth, following its weather patterns, monitoring the environment, searching for oil and minerals, or even spying on countries. Others are used by astronomers to look out at the stars. The most popular use of space, however, is for communication. In 1945, the writer Arthur C. Clarke predicted that we would communicate via space. This was before the silicon chip was invented, and Clarke imagined vast space stations with teams of engineers to service the unreliable, bulky equipment.

△ *In 1962,* Telstar *relayed the first live transatlantic TV transmission, which lasted for 20 minutes.*

△ *The Global Positioning System (GPS) uses the signals from at least three satellites to calculate any position on land or at sea.*

▽ *The giant radio dish at Goonhilly Downs, Cornwall was used to pick up the first transatlantic satellite links.*

Staying in touch

One of the most popular satellite orbits is called geostationary orbit, 22,400 miles (36,000 km) above the equator. Here, satellites orbit at the same speed as the Earth rotates, and so always appear to be overhead. But the distance is so great that either a big dish is needed to receive a satellite's signal, or the signal must be concentrated in a single, powerful beam. Now, networks of satellites are launched into low orbits, so there is always one in range of the hand-held receiver of a mobile phone.

△ *The main satellite orbits around Earth are: low Earth orbit (orange), polar orbit (blue), elliptical or Molniya orbit (green), and geostationary orbit (red).*

△ *In 1997, Tony Bullimore spent five days beneath the hull of his capsized yacht. He was saved when satellites located his radio distress signal.*

Space junk

As more and more rockets and satellites are launched, unwanted junk accumulates in space. Space junk ranges from dropped wrenches and chips of paint to spent rocket motors and defunct satellites. The U.S. Air Force is tracking over 8,500 large objects, but even small pieces can be dangerous—a space shuttle window was once chipped, probably by a flake of paint. Operators are encouraged to relocate old satellites in unused orbits, or force them to burn up in the atmosphere.

▷ Polar orbit is a good place from which to watch the Earth. It is low enough to see detail and, as the Earth rotates beneath a satellite, each orbit surveys a new track. Polar orbit is used by craft such as LandSat *and* ERS 1.

△ *Low Earth orbit is the easiest and cheapest to reach, lying just above the atmosphere, a few hundred miles up. This is the orbit that is taken by the space shuttle, the* Mir *space station, and the* Hubble Space Telescope.

△ *Geostationary orbit, 22,400 miles (36,000 km) above the equator, is commonly used by communications satellites. They orbit over the same point on the Earth so the receivers can be fixed, and can reach a third of the planet at one time.*

◁ *The highly elliptical Molniya orbit was pioneered by Russia. Satellites speed over the low part of their orbit, then hang for a long time over one area as they head farther out to space. The x-ray astronomy satellite ExoSat* (below) *uses this orbit to avoid the Earth's radiation belts.*

Space factories

Spacecraft in a stable orbit are effectively always in microgravity, or weightlessness. This makes them ideal laboratories for studying the effects of weightlessness on, for example, the human body, plants, animals, and delicate materials. The ability to make very pure materials and grow complex crystals in space could also have important applications in medicine and the manufacture of semiconductors used in microelectronics.

▷ *Wherever you are in the world, it is possible to keep in touch using a satellite phone. Originally, this technology was developed for the military and shipping. Now it is used by journalists, businesses, aid workers, and other travelers.*

▷ *The Earth is ringed by a cosmic necklace of satellites, watching over it from a range of different orbits.*

Earthwatch

Strangely, we sometimes need to go into space to see our own world more clearly. From the perspective of space it is possible to see the overall pattern without being confused by detail. As long ago as 1948, the astronomer Fred Hoyle commented that "when a photograph of Earth, taken from outside, is returned, an idea as powerful as any in history will be let loose." To a great extent, he was right. Astronauts comment on how fragile the Earth appears from space. Scientists use observations to build up a picture of the complex systems on the Earth and how our environment is changing. Satellite pictures can inspire a sense of wonder, which may generate a new ecological awareness. Space also provides a window for monitoring military activities, along with disaster relief, peacekeeping, and humanitarian operations.

△ *From low polar orbit,* Landsat 4 *passes over all points on the Earth. This false-color image shows an area of cleared rain forest in Brazil with its network of roads.*

△ *Meteosats hang in geostationary orbit above the Atlantic watching weather systems such as this hurricane forming. This* Meteosat Second Generation Craft *is designed to help forecasters predict weather in the new millennium.*

△ *The ERS-2 satellite measures ozone in the upper atmosphere. Here an ozone hole (in blue) is clearly seen above the Antarctic.*

And now for the weather ...

Satellite images are used in weather forecasts to show us what weather to expect. Weather satellites monitor wind speed, cloud temperature and height, sea temperature, and many other factors. Computers then produce detailed forecasts up to a week ahead. These are vital to farmers, sailors, and even ice-cream makers. This data can also help predict climate changes, such as global warming, decades into the future.

△ *The space shuttle sometimes carries remote sensing instruments for monitoring the Earth. These two images were taken by cloud-penetrating radar. They reveal new flows of ash and lava on Mount Pinotubo, an active volcano in the Philippines.*

△ ERS *satellites use radar, ultraviolet, and infrared to monitor the Earth. Here, two combined images show ground movements after an earthquake.*

△ *Spy satellites often use powerful telescopes to watch for potential threats. Here, a train carrying Iraqi tanks can be seen heading toward Kuwait in 1994.*

Mapping the Earth

In a few 90-minute-long orbits, a satellite can produce a geological survey of an area of remote and mountainous country that would take years to map on the ground. By looking at the ground, not in just the few colors our eyes can see but using hundreds of different bands of the spectrum, it is possible to reveal mineral deposits, polluted areas, and analyze rocks and soil. Satellites can reveal deforestation or the health of crops. They even measure rocks deep inside the Earth in the search for new oil fields.

Spy in the sky

One of the first uses of space was for military purposes. Many rockets were developed to deliver long-range missiles, and more spy satellites may have been launched than any other type. Many take photographs, others monitor radio messages or look for signs of missile launches or bomb tests. In the 1980s, the United States planned a space-based defense system, called "Star Wars." Before the technology and finance could be resolved, the Cold War ended and the project was canceled.

1 2 3

△ *The Solar System took shape from a cloud of gas and dust. A knot of gas begins to pull other gas around it (1). The cloud heats up, and, as it rotates, it contracts and forms into a disk. Energy is lost in jets of matter from the poles (2).*

△ *A protostar gradually forms at the center (3). Secondary knots of gas appear in the disk. These will later become giant gas planets: Jupiter, Saturn, Uranus, and Neptune.*

4

△ *Nuclear processes start up in the star (4). Radiation drives gas and ice out of the inner regions of the disk.*

5

The Solar System

The Solar System is dominated by the Sun, our local star. The Sun is circled by nine planets and their moons, together with countless asteroids and comets. The four planets closest to the Sun—Mercury, Venus, Earth, and Mars—are small, rocky worlds. The next four planets—Jupiter, Saturn, Uranus, and Neptune—are huge and composed of gas. Finally comes Pluto, the smallest of the planets, with a diameter of 1,367 miles (2,200 km). Jupiter is the largest, with a diameter of almost 88,860 miles (143,000 km). But the Sun dwarfs everything else in the Solar System. If the Sun were the size of a soccer ball, then Earth would be smaller than a pea in comparison. Even if all the matter in all the planets were gathered together into a single ball, you could still fit 700 planets inside the Sun and have room to spare.

△ *The Solar System is nearly formed. The Sun is beginning to shine strongly through its still, dusty shroud (5). Planets have formed, but the building rubble is still flying around and bombarding the planets.*

Dusty birthplace

About five billion years ago, the material that now makes up the Sun and planets was a great cloud of gas and dust, called the solar nebula. This material was composed of a mixture of light elements, mostly hydrogen and helium, that had been left over from the formation of our Milky Way Galaxy, and heavier elements spewed out by an earlier generation of short-lived stars. A shock wave may have passed through the nebula as it crossed a spiral arm of the galaxy, or as a nearby star exploded. As a result, the nebula began to condense into a nursery of stars.

◁ *The inclined orbit of Pluto, along with those of Neptune, Uranus, Saturn, and Jupiter, is are clearly visible. Much closer in are the inner planets—Mars, Earth, Venus, and Mercury.*

6

From grains to planets

In one of the protostars, material concentrated to form
the protoSun. Gas and dust around it collected into a flat,
rotating disk. Over the next thousand years, the disk
cooled, and grains of solid matter began to freeze. In
the hot inner region, they were silicate rock; farther out,
frozen water, and even farther, frozen methane. The
grains came together into lumps a few miles across,
which bumped into one another, sometimes breaking
up, but sometimes merging to form the planets.

Leftovers

The newly formed planets mopped up most of the
remaining lumps and grains. The rest of the gas
was blown clear as nuclear processes began in the
Sun, sending a gust of atoms out into space. In
the outermost reaches of the solar nebula, the icy
protoplanetary material was spread so thinly that
it did not form planets, but remains to this day
a vast cloud of potential comets.

▷ *Here, the Sun and planets are shown to scale.*
The Sun dwarfs everything else in the Solar System,
including Jupiter and Saturn.

△ *For the past four billion*
years, little has changed (6).
The Sun has brightened
slightly, a few comets and
asteroids have crashed,
but the nine planets have
remained in stable orbits.
Only Earth has changed
significantly as life
developed on its surface.

NEPTUNE
URANUS
PLUTO
JUPITER
MERCURY
VENUS
EARTH
MARS
SATURN

Mercury

Mercury, named after the Roman winged messenger of the gods, is an elusive planet. Small, fast-moving, and lying closer to the Sun than any other planet, it is only visible from the Earth just after sunset or just before dawn. Mercury is the second smallest planet and only slightly larger than our Moon. It takes just 88 Earth days to orbit the Sun. Its distance from the Sun varies from 29 million miles (46 million km) at its closest to 43 million miles (70 million km) at its most distant. The Sun's strong gravitational tug on Mercury has dramatically slowed the planet's rotation on its axis. This has the result that a day on Mercury lasts the equivalent of 176 Earth days—twice as long as its quicksilver 88-day year.

△ *Almost everything we know about Mercury comes from one space probe,* Mariner 10, *which flew past the planet in 1973, 1974, and again in 1975. Here,* Mariner 10 *is shown above a false-color image of Mercury's cratered surface.*

▽ *Mercury's dry and airless surface creates a very bleak landscape. Pockmarked with impact craters, during the day it is baked by radiation and heat from the nearby Sun.*

Unchanged features

The surface of Mercury is very similar to the Moon's. It is heavily cratered, with evidence of ancient lava flows. With no atmosphere or water to erode them, the craters look almost as fresh as the day they formed. Yet that must have been more than 4 billion years ago, when debris left over from the formation of the planets was still flying around in the Solar System. This rubble crashed into the surface, throwing up circular craters with characteristic central peaks.

△ *There is evidence from radar on Earth that there may be ice in craters near Mercury's poles. In deep craters, icy deposits— possibly leftover material from comet impacts— would remain hidden from the Sun's intense heat.*

World of extremes

Mercury has no atmosphere (except for a trace of helium given off by the rocks), so there is no wind or rain. There is also no protection against the Sun's searing heat by day, and no blanket to keep the surface warm at night. Days and nights each last about three Earth months. With the planet swinging closer and farther from the Sun, temperatures can range from 788°F (420°C) to −292°F (−180°C). These extremes are hot enough to melt some metals or cold enough to freeze air.

△ *Although only about a third the size of the Earth, Mercury is almost as dense. This suggests that a core of iron-nickel takes up about 70 percent of the interior, with a mantle of silicate rock surrounding it. The outer part of the metal core may still be molten.*

◁ △ *More than four billion years ago, a huge object must have struck Mercury* (above), *melting part of the surface and causing ridges and hills to form on the opposite side of the planet. The ridges around the impact crater, called the Caloris Basin* (left), *were photographed by* Mariner 10.

Wizened world

A surprise discovery by *Mariner 10* was a magnetic field on Mercury. The planet had been thought to rotate too slowly for it to generate a magnetic field. The answer may lie in the planet's large core. If the outer part is still molten, currents in it could produce a weak magnetic effect. A big iron core could also explain Mercury's wrinkles. As it cooled and solidified, the iron shrank, making the planet contract and producing a wrinkled appearance on the surface.

Venus

△ *Bands of thick, swirling clouds circle Venus at speeds of up to 225 mph (360 km/hr). This ultraviolet picture was taken by* Mariner 10 *in 1974.*

Venus, the brightest planet visible from Earth, is named after the goddess of beauty. The planet has also been called the Earth's twin. It is almost exactly the same size, is only slightly less dense, and is made up of volcanic rocks, but there the similarity ends. The thick atmosphere on Venus means that it is always cloudy, and the pressure on the surface is 90 times greater than on Earth. The dense atmosphere consists mostly of carbon dioxide, and this traps the planet's heat, causing a runaway greenhouse effect that makes the worst predictions of global warming on Earth seem chilly by comparison. The surface temperature is 896°F (480°C), and if oceans ever existed on Venus they have long since boiled away. If you could withstand the searing heat and bone-crushing pressure on this hostile planet, you would see an orange sky. If it ever rained, you would be drenched in a lethal downpour of sulfuric acid.

△ *Four Russian Venera probes have landed on Venus and sent back images. In 1982, close-ups taken by* Venera 13 *revealed flat, eroded terrain southeast of a volcanic region called Phoebe Regio. The edge of the Venus lander and its lens cap can also be seen in the picture.*

△ *The* Magellan *radar mapper revealed that the surface of Venus has rough, mountainous terrain (bright areas) and smoother plains (darker areas).*

Global warming

The dramatic contrast with the Earth could simply be because Venus is closer to the Sun. As the young Sun warmed, more carbon dioxide was released from volcanoes and the surface temperature climbed. The seas began to evaporate, the water vapor adding to the greenhouse effect. Without oceans and plants, carbon dioxide could not be removed as the heat output of the Sun continued to grow. On the Earth, billions of tons of carbon are locked up in limestone and chalk. On Venus it is all still in the atmosphere.

Revealing geology

The radar mapper on the *Magellan* space probe indicated clear evidence of volcanic activity, including domes of thick or viscous lava and vast floods of liquid basalt. However, it did not detect any drifting plates, which on Earth create great chains of volcanoes. There must be other forces at work on Venus, still to be identified.

▽ *The background landscape is a computer-generated view of Maat Mons, 5 miles (8 km) high and one of the largest volcanoes on Venus. This image was created by data sent back by the* Magellan *probe. Fresh lava flows around the volcano suggest that it is still active.*

▷ *The* Magellan *probe, seen here as it was released from the space shuttle in 1989, was made up of spare parts from other missions.*

△ *The existence of uneroded craters on Venus indicates that some parts of the surface are much older than areas covered by volcanic lava. The largest crater (top left) has a diameter of 30 miles (50 km).*

△ *This corona, or circular feature, is 125 miles (200 km) across. It was probably caused by a rising dome of lava from deep below the surface.*

△ *Like the Earth, Venus has a rocky mantle and a crust. Inside is an iron core that may be partly molten. Because the planet rotates very slowly (unlike the Earth), there is no noticeable magnetic field.*

◁ *The atmosphere of Venus is 96 percent carbon dioxide. Nitrogen, water vapor, and traces of gases such as sulfur dioxide are also present.*

Lengthy days

Venus is best seen from Earth with the naked eye just after sunset or before dawn. Like the Moon, Venus has phases as the Sun illuminates a crescent, half, or full disk. Venus has a slow rotation from east to west. In fact, its rotation rate of 243 Earth days makes a day on Venus longer than the planet's year—the time it takes to revolve once around the Sun.

The Earth

△ The Earth was formed from the solar nebula. Before the atmosphere formed, impacts made it a hot, volcanic planet.

△ Charged particles from the Sun rain down near the Earth's poles, creating the spectacular Northern and Southern Lights, or aurora.

The Earth is the planet we call home. Almost every astronaut who has seen it from space has been deeply moved by its fragile beauty, and its thin veil of white cloud and blue haze. Even alien observers would recognize that the Earth is special. The presence of liquid water oceans, ice caps, and clouds of water vapor suggests a narrow range of temperatures that are just right for life. An abundance of life using photosynthesis to trap carbon dioxide and release oxygen ensures that levels of oxygen and ozone in the atmosphere remain stable. Without this process, the greenhouse effect would spiral out of control. The Earth is a planet that teems with living things and is largely controlled by them.

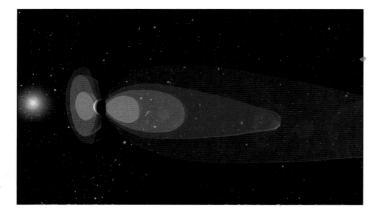

△ The Earth plows through the solar wind like a ship, its magnetic field extending into surrounding space. This magnetic envelope, or magnetosphere, is pushed up into a wave in front and trails a long wake.

The young Earth

Around 4.6 billion years ago, the early Earth may have had a thick atmosphere, but the solar wind and intense heat of meteorite impacts soon stripped this away. The interior separated into a metallic core, a thick mantle of silicate rocks, and a crust of lighter silicates. Once the surface had cooled down, a rain of comets probably provided most of the water now in our oceans.

▷ On the Earth all three forms of water (ice, liquid, and vapor) are found. Together, they help provide a climate that is just right for life.

△ *Beneath a thin silicate crust, the Earth has a solid rocky mantle, an outer core of molten iron, and a solid iron inner core. When the thin ocean crust dives back down into the mantle, it triggers volcanic eruptions* (above right).

▷ *The Earth's atmosphere extends out more than 62 miles (100 km). It is made up of 77 percent nitrogen, 21 percent oxygen, and a small amount of other gases.*

Life appears

The first primitive life forms may have developed in shallow pools, or perhaps around hydrothermal vents. Life may even have been seeded from space on fragments of meteorites, or comets. Soon, bacteria and viruses were joined by algae, which began to transform the atmosphere by using up carbon dioxide and releasing oxygen. Finally, more than four billion years later, intelligent life developed.

Below the crust

The inside of the Earth is still hot. The molten outer core of iron generates electrical currents that produce the planet's magnetic field. The bulk of the planet, the mantle, is silicate rock. It is solid but hot, and is able to distort and flow a little like ice in a glacier. The continents float and drift on the mantle. Where the mantle is hottest, it rises and forms new ocean crust. The ocean floor cools and eventually sinks back into the mantle. All this means that the entire surface of the Earth is made up of a series of plates, edged with volcanoes and earthquake zones.

△ *The Earth is a medium-sized planet with a thick atmosphere. Great stretches of water cover three-quarters of the surface.*

△ *Europe's four Cluster probes fly in formation through the Earth's magnetosphere, plotting the planet's interactions with the solar wind.*

The Moon

The Moon is the most spectacular object in the night sky, and it is the only world beyond Earth so far on which people have walked. It is our closest neighbor, orbiting our planet with the same face always pointing toward us. The far side is often called the dark side, because it cannot be seen from Earth. In its monthly orbit, the Moon seems to change shape as different areas of its surface are lit by the Sun. The Moon's five distinct phases are called new, crescent, quarter, gibbous, and full. When the side we see is dark (a new Moon), the far side is in full sunshine. The Moon is close enough to the Earth for its gravity to pull the water in our oceans toward it, causing the tides.

△ *This mosaic of 1,500 images shows the south pole of the Moon. The dark crater in the center is permanently in shade and contains an icy layer.*

△ *Craters were formed when asteroids plunged into the lunar surface. They can be anything from a few yards to hundreds of miles across.*

How the Moon formed

There are several theories to explain how the Moon formed. It may have formed together with the Earth from the solar nebula, or perhaps it spun off from a bulge at the Earth's equator. The most popular theory, derived from analysis of Moon rock and computer simulations, is that the early Earth was hit by a protoplanet the size of Mars. Some of the resulting debris merged to form the Moon.

△ *This view of the Moon's craters, lit by sunlight at a low angle, was taken from* Apollo 13 *in 1970.*

▷ *The five different phases of the Moon depend on the direction from which it is illuminated by the Sun. During each monthly cycle it goes through nine different stages.*

▷ *On the left is the Moon as seen from Earth, with its highlands and dark, flat* maria. *On the right is part of the heavily cratered far*

The Moon's surface

The lunar highlands are more than 4.2 billion years old and heavily cratered. Collisions with asteroids were violent enough to melt parts of the Moon's surface, flooding the impact basins with lava and creating great dark regions called *maria*, or seas. Strangely, there are almost no such features on the far side of the Moon. About 3.8 billion years ago, the asteroid bombardment virtually ceased, aside from the creation of a few craters such as Copernicus. Without wind and water to erode the surface, the Moon has remained the same ever since.

NEW MOON

WAXING CRESCENT

FIRST QUARTER

WAXING GIBBOUS

▷ *The Moon was probably formed 4.5 billion years ago when a rocky protoplanet as big as Mars crashed into the newly formed Earth. Both bodies became molten, and their cores merged.*

▷ *The vaporized rock and fragments from the collision formed a ring around the Earth. Some of the material combined to make an object massive enough to sweep up the debris with its gravity. Finally, only two bodies remained in this area of the Solar System—the Earth and its new Moon.*

Tomorrow's Moon

Twelve men have walked on the Moon, leaving landers, rovers, flags, and footprints behind. And it is still the goal of many scientists and commercial enterprises. With only one-sixth of the Earth's gravity, the Moon would be a very good place to mine bulk materials for launch into space. With permanently dark skies, no atmosphere, and no radio noise, it would also be an excellent site for setting up telescopes. Water, discovered frozen in the rocks of the south pole, could be used to supply moonbases. The main obstacle, at the moment, is the cost.

◁ *The Moon's low gravity would make moonbases good staging posts for interplanetary journeys in the future. And its airless surface and dark skies would make an excellent laboratory for astronomers and scientists.*

FULL MOON **WANING GIBBOUS** **LAST QUARTER** **WANING CRESCENT** **OLD MOON**

△ *There is a thin crust of light colored, granitelike rock on the highlands of the Moon, above a thick, dark, and dense rocky mantle.*

Mars

Mars is smaller, darker, and slightly more distant than Venus. It is also the most Earthlike of the planets and has always attracted humans. Mars's reddish color (with its associations of blood) led to it being named after the Roman god of war, and Martians have featured in countless science fiction stories. Speculation about life on Mars was reinforced by changing hues on the surface and reported sightings of canals. When the first Mariner probes flew past in the 1960s, however, all they saw was a barren, cratered surface, somewhat like the Moon, beneath an atmosphere one hundredth the density of the Earth's. In 1971, *Mariner 9* (the first craft to orbit a planet other than the Earth) explored Mars's fascinating geology. As the dust from a violent storm settled, a giant volcano was revealed, followed by valleys and canyons.

△ *This picture of Mars was taken by the* Hubble Space Telescope *in 1990. It reveals wispy storm clouds around the north pole and thin dust clouds in the south.*

△ *The* Mars Global Surveyor *arrived at Mars in September 1997 to begin mapping the planet with high resolution cameras, lasers, and radar.*

◁ *Mars has two tiny moons, Phobos* (top) *and Deimos* (bottom). *Both are probably captured asteroids. Phobos is heavily cratered. Deimos is smoother and darker.*

Heat and dust

Like Earth, Mars has a 24-hour day, although its year is nearly twice as long. The thin atmosphere is made almost entirely of carbon dioxide. Cloud swirls are often visible and, in winter, polar caps of water ice and frozen carbon dioxide form. Temperatures range from a comfortable 77°F (25°C) in summer to a bitter −184°F (−120°C) on winter nights. Although it no longer rains, there is clear evidence that water once flowed on Mars, scouring out deep channels. Today, strong winds whip up dust storms, which sometimes envelop the whole planet.

△ *Mars has a weak magnetic field, suggesting that its core must be solid. The thick rocky mantle may circulate slowly beneath a thin, hard crust.*

◁ *The Martian atmosphere is only one hundredth the density of the Earth's. Although it is 95 percent carbon dioxide, it does little to insulate the planet.*

◁ *Two Viking Landers touched down on Mars in 1976. The sampling arm (front left) scooped up soil for analysis. The two cylinders with vertical slits are stereo cameras.*

▷ *Unlike Mars's south pole, which is mostly frozen carbon dioxide, its north pole is mostly water ice. Every summer it shrinks, leaving a spiral pattern, probably due to wind erosion.*

▷ *Evidence shows that water once flowed down this valley in the Valles Marineris.*

▷ *Lava flows on the flanks of the volcano Alba Patera produced this unusual pattern, photographed by Viking 2's orbiter.*

△ *The Ophir Chasm, in the Valles Marineris, was formed by geological faulting. Its 13,000-foot (4,000-m) cliffs have seen major landslides, including an avalanche that traveled 40 miles (65 km).*

△ *The biggest volcano on Mars, and in the Solar System, is Olympus Mons at 86,600 feet (26,400 m) high. Like the Earth's biggest volcanoes, it is shield shaped, and once erupted runny, black, basalt lava.*

Vikings invade Mars

By the 1970s, it was clear that Mars was neither covered in lush vegetation nor populated by Martians. But there might be microscopic life (bacteria or algae) in the soil. In 1976, two Viking space probes set out to investigate. Each comprised an orbiter and a lander. Both landers contained miniature laboratories to test Martian soil samples for signs of life. They fed nutrients into the soil and, when a gas was given off, this suggested that living organisms were using up the nutrients. But the process slowed and stopped. Scientists concluded that all they had detected were lifeless chemical reactions.

The Martian landscape

Some parts of Mars are heavily cratered and very old. Other parts have been smoothed over by newer lava flows from volcanoes. Cracks and canyons indicate past earthquakes. The Valles Marineris (*below*) is four times deeper and six times wider than the Grand Canyon in the United States. It has large areas of windblown sand dunes. Dust storms change the surface dramatically, covering or exposing rock underneath. Signs of water erosion suggest past flooding along channels and plains. This water may have escaped to space or lie frozen underground.

△ *A panorama taken by Viking 2 in the Utopia Planitia region. The sloping ground is strewn with angular lumps of dark, volcanic rock and frosted with a thin layer of water ice.*

Mission to Mars

The year 1997 marked the return to the red planet. For almost twenty years, every Mars mission ended in failure. The two Russian *Phobos* crafts failed, the U.S. *Mars Observer* exploded as it prepared to enter the planet's orbit, and the mighty Russian *Mars '96* craft did not escape from the Earth's atmosphere. But finally, on Independence Day, 1997, *Mars Pathfinder* parachuted down to Mars, and its new landing technology proved to be a success. A little six-wheeled rover, *Sojourner*, spent nearly three months analyzing Martian rocks before the battery went flat. More missions have been planned, including a mission to return rock samples to Earth, and ultimately one to land the first humans on Mars.

△ *As* Mars Pathfinder *neared the surface, the tether to its parachute was cut and balloons inflated. The craft bounced to a standstill and opened up to reveal instruments, solar cells, and a little rover* (inset below).

Where did all the water go?

Great floods of water once washed down from the Martian highlands and fanned out onto the plains below. Now all the water has escaped to space, or lies frozen underground, or in the icecaps. For water to flow, Mars must once have been warmer, with a denser atmosphere. About three billion years ago all that changed. The once-molten iron core may have solidified, or the planet may have been struck by an asteroid. Whatever the cause, it resulted in the cold, barren world we see today.

Meteorite from Mars

In 1984, a grapefruit-sized lump of rock was found in Antarctica. After years of careful research, scientists were able to tell its story. It had formed on Mars 4.5 billion years ago, when the planet was still young. Then, 16 million years ago, an impact threw it out into space, and 13,000 years ago, it landed on Earth. The meteorite contains chemicals and microscopic structures that some NASA scientists suggest are evidence of life—fossils from another world.

▽ Mars Pathfinder *landed in a wide flood plain. The camera revealed a panorama of low hills and a surface littered with rocks of all sizes and textures for the rover* Sojourner *to analyze.*

▷ *A Martian hand reaches out from a spaceship in the* film *The War of the Worlds.*

◁ Sojourner *used an x-ray spectrometer to measure the composition of rocks. Here, it is examining the rock given the name "Barnacle Bill."*

◁ *The six-wheeled* Sojourner, *the size of a microwave oven, moved from rock to rock, navigating with its own camera and laser, as well as instructions from Earth.*

△ *AH84001* (left) *is a Martian meteorite that was found in Antarctica. It contains possible fossil evidence of life. Under a powerful electron microscope, a segment of rock reveals structures that could be tiny fossil bacteria* (above).

▽ *In the distant future, Mars may be made more Earthlike. A thicker atmosphere and warmer climate will allow liquid water to remain on the surface—just as it did some four billion years ago.*

Alien invaders

Evidence on Earth suggests that life can endure extremes of temperature and even survive in cracks within rocks. Although Mars appears to be a barren planet, life may once have thrived there in similarly hostile conditions. Fossil hunters of the future will want to explore any ancient hydrothermal springs they may find on Mars. Returned samples are likely to be put into quarantine— just in case microbes are still alive and choose to invade the Earth!

Home from home

Sending people to Mars—and returning them to Earth—might be more feasible if the fuel for the return journey were to be made on Mars. A robot craft could make propellant from the Martian atmosphere before astronauts arrived. A more fantastic idea is using orbiting mirrors to warm the south pole of Mars. This would release more carbon dioxide and warm the planet. Bacteria might release oxygen and ultimately make the atmosphere breathable for human colonists.

△ *On June 30, 1908, a huge fireball flattened 1,200 sq. miles (3,000 sq. km) of forest near Tunguska, Siberia. It was probably caused by an asteroid exploding in the atmosphere.*

▽ *The asteroid belt, between Mars and Jupiter, contains rocks of all sizes. Although they frequently collide and break up, the belt is made up mostly of empty space. All together, the asteroids would form an object smaller than the Moon.*

Asteroids & Meteorites

Between the orbits of Mars and Jupiter is a gigantic belt made up of more than 4,000 lumps of rock. They range in size from several feet across to the biggest, called Ceres, which is about 620 miles (1,000 km) across. These chunks of rock are called asteroids. Scientists believe they were formed from material similar to that of the rocky planets, such as the Earth and Mars. Stirred up by the immense gravitational influence of Jupiter, this material was unable to stick together to form a single planet. However, mini planets with iron cores may have formed, only to be smashed up by impacts with smaller debris. Collisions between asteroids are thought to be frequent. Some of the asteroids are composed mostly of iron, like the core of the Earth.

◁ *When a 19-mile (30-km) asteroid hit Central America 65 million years ago, it caused a huge fireball and climate change that may have ended the age of the dinosaurs. A map (inset) of Mexico's Yucatan Peninsula shows the crater left by the impact.*

A big impact

Not all asteroids remain in orbit between Jupiter and Mars. Some have elliptical orbits that bring them close to the Earth. Craters on the Moon were caused by asteroid impacts. Evidence of asteroids bombarding Earth has mostly worn away, but geologists have identified traces of enormous ancient craters. One, in the Gulf of Mexico, was caused by an asteroid 19 miles (30 km) across that fell 65 million years ago. It threw up thousands of tons of water and rock, blocking out the Sun and contributing to the extinction of the dinosaurs.

Could it happen again?

Occasionally, asteroid-sized rocks still hit the Earth. Small asteroids strike once every 100 years, probably over uninhabited land or sea. A 1-mile (2-km)-sized object may hit only once in a million years, but it could change the climate and, indirectly, kill millions of people. Telescopes now look out for rocks that pose a threat, in the hope that missiles or lasers can be used to deflect them.

▷ *Wolf Creek crater* (above) *in Western Australia was formed about 10,000 years ago and still looks fresh. Deep Bay* (below) *in Reindeer Lake, Canada, is 150 million years old. It is so eroded that it was not thought to be an impact crater until 1957.*

Meteorites

Hundreds of tons of rock hit the Earth each year, but most burn up in the atmosphere to form shooting stars. Lumps that reach the surface are called meteorites. A few are chips off comets, the Moon, or even Mars, but most are asteroid debris. Collectors scour Australia and Antarctica to recover them. Even the bigger ones, which vaporize on impact, leave traces. They can enrich sediments many miles away with the element iridium.

△ *The most common meteorites are stony ones made of silicate rocks* (1). *Glassy tektites* (2) *form on impact from vaporized rock. Meteorites made of iron* (3 and 4) *are more rare.*

△ *Small metallic asteroids may be very valuable due to the iron, copper, cobalt, and nickel they contain. This imaginary scene shows one captured for mining in orbit around Earth.*

◁ *Under the microscope, a thin slice of meteorite reveals its component minerals. Crystals formed at high temperatures are surrounded by dark material formed at lower temperatures.*

Jupiter

Jupiter is the giant among
the planets. If all the others
were combined they still would not
add up to half of Jupiter's mass. It is a
great gas bag made up of 90 percent hydrogen
with a lower density than the Earth. Down in its thick atmosphere, the
pressure rises to a point where hydrogen behaves as a liquid rather than
a gas. Deeper still, it is like a liquid metal, with huge, circulating electrical
currents. Here, a powerful magnetic field is generated, strong enough
to emit radio noise that can be received on the Earth. Jupiter is still
contracting from its formation, a process that generates heat and makes it
glow in the infrared. If Jupiter were much bigger, the heating would
start nuclear fusion in its core, and the planet would become a star.

△ *This ultraviolet
image shows the glow
at Jupiter's poles, as
charged particles from
the Sun stream along
its magnetic field lines.*

△ *This photo shows Jupiter's
thin rings, as seen by* Voyager 2
*from a distance of 901,030
miles (1,450,000 km).*

Turbulent planet

Jupiter's incredibly fast 9 hour and 55 minute rotation
(or day) makes it bulge 5,592 miles (9,000 km) wider at its
equator than its poles. It whips up violent winds and stretches
the clouds into bands parallel to the equator. Essentially,
there are about 14 alternating bands of dark, low pressure
regions that circulate with the planet's rotation, and light,
high pressure regions that blow the other way. Swirling storm
systems form where they meet, especially in the turbulent
polar regions. High, white clouds of ammonia ice are tinted
yellow and orange lower down by sulfur compounds.

△ *The red bands in this
infrared image are gases
from the deeper atmosphere,
heated by the planet's
continued contraction.*

◁ Voyager 2 *went on a grand tour of the giant planets, passing Jupiter in 1979, Saturn in 1981, Uranus in 1986, and Neptune in 1989.*

Cosmic fireworks

In 1993, comet hunters David Levy and Gene and Carolyn Shoemaker spotted a strange comet. It had come so close to Jupiter that gravitational forces had torn it into what looked like a long string of pearls. Calculations showed that the fragments would crash into Jupiter (*left*) in July 1994. No one knew what to expect. The impacts would be just out of sight over Jupiter's horizon, so perhaps nothing would be seen. In fact, the fireballs were clearly visible and, when the impact sites rotated into view, they appeared as great brown marks, larger than the Earth.

△ *The Red Spot, a 24,856-mile (40,000-km) storm system, has been raging for over 300 years. It has a dramatic effect on surrounding weather systems* (inset). *Nearby white ovals are huge temporary storms.*

Visitors to Jupiter

Five spacecraft have visited Jupiter. *Pioneer 10* and *11* and *Voyager 1* and *2* sped past, giving valuable but tantalizingly brief glimpses. (*Voyager* discovered a thin ring of particles as fine as smoke.) But in December 1995, *Galileo* went into orbit around the giant planet. On arrival, it released a probe that descended into Jupiter's atmosphere before being destroyed by the heat. The probe found less water than was expected, but it may just have missed the moist clouds. Although the spacecraft's main antenna failed to open properly, *Galileo* has still returned spectacular pictures and data.

△ *Jupiter's clouds lie in a thin layer on the surface. Below this, the atmosphere of hydrogen and helium is compressed until it behaves like a liquid metal. Inside is a compressed rocky core, slightly bigger than the Earth.*

△ *The southern part of Jupiter, photographed in July 1994 by the* Hubble Space Telescope. *Dark chemicals welling up from deep in the atmosphere mark the impact sites of fragments of comet* Shoemaker Levy 9. *Each mark lasted for several months.*

◁ *The highest clouds in the atmosphere are made of white ammonia ice crystals. Deeper down, they are tinged with sulfur compounds made from traces of hydrogen sulfide. Even deeper may be water vapor clouds like those on Earth.*

Jupiter's Moons

△ A faint greenish light penetrates cracks in the ice. Some scientists think that under the ice there could even be liquid water.

When Galileo first looked at Jupiter through his telescope in January 1610, he saw three, then four, tiny starlike objects moving close to the planet. He quickly realized that these were moons orbiting Jupiter. Each of these moons—Callisto, Ganymede, Europa, and Io—is a world in its own right. We now know of 12 other moons. These include four that orbit inside Galileo's moons. Beyond them lie four more, 7 million miles (11 million km) from Jupiter. Finally, at twice that distance, are another four. These may have been passing asteroids, captured by Jupiter's gravity.

△ *The orange, sulfurous surface of Io is churned up by Jupiter's gravity, resulting in these fresh lava flows from a volcanic crater. The volcanic gases escape into space to form a ring around Jupiter.*

Callisto and Ganymede

Callisto is the same size as Mercury and is covered almost entirely with craters. One huge impact structure, called Valhalla, consists of rings up to 1,900 miles (3,000 km) across. Its dark, dirty crust is a mixture of ice and rock and may be 190 miles (300 km) deep, with water or slush lying underneath. Ganymede is the largest moon in the Solar System at 3,279 miles (5,276 km) across. Its icy surface has large, dark patches that are heavily cratered. Ganymede's magnetic field raises the possibility that it still has an active interior.

◁ *The grooved surface of Ganymede appears to be made up of separate slabs of icy material.*

The mystery of Europa

Europa is only 948 miles (1,525 km) across, but it could turn out to be the most exciting of Jupiter's moons. The smooth, white surface has very few craters, but is crazed by numerous cracks. The cracks look very similar to those in pack ice on Earth. This suggests that the ice is floating on an ocean of liquid water. Hydrothermal vents in the ocean floor might provide energy as they do on Earth, and it is just possible that life could have developed in the cold, dark water.

Io, world of fire

Io is the most volcanically active world in the Solar System. It is tugged so hard by Jupiter's gravity that tidal forces churn up the surface and interior, keeping the moon partly molten. The Voyager craft saw eruptions taking place, with sulfur dioxide spewing 190 miles (300 km) up into space. Other volcanoes have left dark lava flows and red and yellow patches of sulfur, making this moon look like a moldy orange.

△ *This composite picture shows Jupiter dwarfing its four main moons. Closest to the great planet is Io (top), followed by Europa, Ganymede—the largest moon—and Callisto.*

◁ *If oceans do exist beneath Europa's icy surface, there is also the possibility of life flourishing in the cold water. Volcanic vents on the ocean floor could provide the energy to support life, whatever form it might take.*

▷ *Callisto's ancient surface is pockmarked by billions of years of impacts.*

△ Voyager 2 *revealed the cracked, icy surface of Europa. In close-up the structures resemble those found in pack ice around the Earth's poles, with tilted slabs, cracks, and icebergs.*

Saturn

fter Galileo discovered Jupiter's moons he turned his attention to what appeared to be a triple planet. Then the objects to the sides seemed to disappear, making him suspect they were gas clouds. It was a Dutch astronomer, Christiaan Huygens, who finally realized, in 1675, that Saturn was a ringed planet. Just under 200 years later it was shown that the rings could not possibly be solid disks, but must be made up of millions of smaller particles of rock or ice, each acting like a tiny moon. When space probes *Pioneer 11* (1979), *Voyager 1* (1980),

△ Voyager 1 *found dark lines running across Saturn's rings, like spokes on a wheel. Since the rings orbit at different speeds, the spokes were difficult to explain. They are now thought to be caused by ice crystals charged with static electricity.*

△ *An image, taken by the* Hubble Space Telescope *in 1990, enhanced to show the clouds. An elongated Great White Spot of ammonia ice crystals has formed high up in the atmosphere. The false colors pick out the top of the spot in red.*

and *Voyager 2* (1981) flew past Saturn, it became clear that there are thousands of separate bands of different densities within the main rings (which are named A, B, C, D, and E). There is also a very thin F ring outside these, its particles kept in line by two tiny moons. The rings are less than 98 feet (30 m) thick, and may have formed from the breakup of a giant comet that strayed too close to Saturn.

Stormy weather

A constant dull yellow haze of high ammonia clouds masks the deeper structure of Saturn's atmosphere. Occasionally, telescopes can make out a huge, swirling, white storm system. Computer enhancement of the Voyager images revealed circulating bands of clouds similar to Jupiter's. The fastest winds race around Saturn's equator, reaching up to 1,100 miles (1,800 km) per hour. To the north and south of the equator are alternating bands of slow and fast winds.

△ As Voyager 2 *drew away from Saturn, it photographed the rings illuminated from behind. By tracking a star as it passed behind the rings, thousands of individual ringlets were recorded.*

▷ *Two pictures of Saturn taken by the* Hubble Space Telescope. *In the top picture, the shadow of the rings and Titan, Saturn's largest moon, are visible. In the bottom picture, Saturn appears with its rings tilted.*

▷ *Voyager 2 was 27 million miles (43 million km) away from Saturn when it recorded this image in 1981. Computers have enhanced the dull yellow clouds to reveal bands in the atmosphere as winds up to 1,100 mph (1,800 km/h) encircle the planet. A double storm system is visible in the southern hemisphere.*

△ *Saturn's atmosphere may be 1,200 miles (2,000 km) deep with liquid hydrogen reaching down another 20,000 miles (32,000 km).*

◁ *Beneath a yellow haze, the Voyager probes identified three layers in Saturn's atmosphere. The outer layer has clouds of ammonia, followed by ammonium sulfide, and finally clouds containing water.*

Planetary structure

Like Jupiter, Saturn does not have a solid surface, although astronomers think it has a small, rocky core at its center. The planet is 75,000 miles (120,000 km) across (without its rings) and 95 times Earth's mass. Hydrogen makes up 94 percent; the rest is helium, with traces of ammonia, methane, and other gases. Also like Jupiter, most of the interior is liquid hydrogen, which deep down becomes an electrically conducting, metallic liquid. Electrical currents here generate a strong magnetic field. A day at the equator lasts a brief 10 hours, 15 minutes.

▷ *During the six-year journey to Saturn, Cassini's trajectory will include two Venus flybys, one flyby of the Earth, and one of Jupiter.*

Last bus to Saturn

Since the Voyager flybys, only one probe has been sent to distant Saturn. *Cassini* is the size of a bus and packed with instruments. Launched in 1997, *Cassini* will arrive in 2004 and go into orbit, surveying the planet, its rings, moons, and magnetic field for at least three years.

Saturn's Moons

Saturn is at the center of a solar system in miniature. Besides the billions of particles making up its rings, 23 different moons have been identified. Some are lumps of rock only a few miles across that lie close to the planet and shepherd the rings into place. Saturn's most distant moon, Phoebe, is nearly 8 million miles (13 million km) from the planet. The biggest of all the moons is Titan. At 3,200 miles (5,150 km) across, it is bigger than Mercury and has a thick atmosphere. It is the only atmosphere astronomers know of, aside from the Earth's, that is made up mostly of nitrogen. The surface of Titan is very cold—about −292°F (−180°C)—and the atmospheric pressure is double that of our own planet. Titan's atmosphere resembles the early Earth's, but kept in frozen lifelessness.

△ *Discovered by Christiaan Huygens in 1655, Titan is the second largest moon in the Solar System.* Voyager 2 *saw only this orange ball of smog, made by the action of sunlight on Titan's atmosphere.*

▽ *High in Titan's nitrogen atmosphere is a layer that absorbs ultraviolet rays. A thin blue haze of carbon chemicals sits above an unbroken layer of orange smog. Below this, the sky may have clouds of methane.*

△ *In November 2004, after a seven-year journey, the* Huygens *probe will be released above the clouds of Titan from the* Cassini *Saturn orbiter. After an initial fiery entry, the heat shield will fall away, and the probe will parachute down to the surface of the moon.*

A giant among moons

The interior of Titan is probably a mixture of rock and ice, with a rocky core that has an ice mantle. The ice could never melt, but there may be lakes or seas on Titan, not of water but of liquid natural gas or methane. Methane rain or snow may fall from the clouds. The Voyager probes were unable to see any features on Titan because it is wrapped in a thick, butterscotch yellow, chemical smog.

Mysterious worlds

Saturn's other large moons are equally strange. Enceladus has an ancient, cratered landscape, with signs of newer activity in the form of smooth plains and a series of ridges. Iapetus, the outermost of Saturn's big moons, is a little denser than water, suggesting it is mostly ice. One side is bright and cratered but the opposite side is as black as anything in the Solar System. Dione has light, wispy markings that may be trails of frost sprayed out from ice volcanoes. Mimas, just outside the rings, has an enormous crater, like a huge black eye. Tethys is made up mostly of pure ice and has a crack, 60 miles (100 km) across and 3 miles (5 km) deep, running almost pole to pole.

Landing on Titan

On November 27, 2004 the *Cassini* Saturn orbiter will release the *Huygens* probe above the clouds of Titan. No one knows what the probe will find. It may land on rock or ice, or even in a sea of liquid methane. If waves do not sink it, the probe will use sonar to measure depths, as well as recording temperatures and composition. It may even find the basic chemicals needed for life, suspended in a deep freeze.

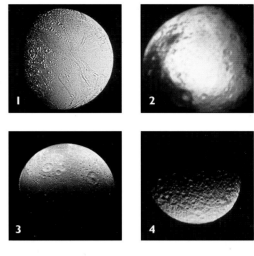

△ *These* Voyager *images show five of Saturn's large moons: Enceladus* (1), *Iapetus* (2), *Dione* (3), *Mimas* (4), *and Tethys* (5).

▽ *The* Huygens *probe will have 2.5 hours to make its readings as it descends through the smog of Titan. It is designed to survive landings on both solid and liquid surfaces.*

Uranus

△ *By using computers to stretch blues and greens into a wider spectrum, scientists were able to see white clouds of methane near Uranus's equator* (top left).

Mercury, Venus, Mars, Jupiter, and Saturn are all visible to the naked eye and have been known since ancient times. Uranus was the first planet to be discovered through a telescope. One March night in 1781, the astronomer William Herschel noticed what he described as "either a nebulous star or perhaps a comet." He actually had become the first person to discover Uranus. Although it is four times the size of the Earth, Uranus is twice as far away as Saturn and, even through a telescope, only appears as a tiny greenish disk. Herschel wanted to name the new planet after the English king, George III, but in the end it was named after Uranus, the Greek god of the sky.

Cloudy world

Only one probe, *Voyager 2*, has visited Uranus, on January 24, 1986. No one knew what it would find, as the planet appears totally featureless through telescopes on the Earth. When the probe's pictures were enhanced, they revealed clouds on the surface. These show that the planet rotates once every 17 hours, 14 minutes, with winds blowing at up to 190 mph (300 km/h).

▽ *Combining images taken by* Voyager 2 *through orange, blue, and green filters revealed Uranus as a featureless blue ball.*

Surprise discovery

In March 1977, astronomers noticed a star passing behind Uranus. Hoping to record how it dimmed as it disappeared behind the atmosphere, they tracked it with an infrared telescope. To their amazement, the star flickered on and off. The only explanation was that Uranus is also encircled by rings.

△ Voyager 2 *confirmed that Uranus has rings, 11 in all, of very dark, boulder-sized fragments. Here, fine dust is revealed between the main rings as they are backlit by the Sun.*

◁ *This color-enhanced picture, taken as* Voyager 2 *approached Uranus's south pole, indicated that a high-altitude haze had formed during the southern hemisphere's 42-year-long summer.*

◁ *Miranda, only 300 miles (480 km) across, has a varied landscape with old, cratered plains and ice cliffs. Regions like the Chevron (below) suggest the moon was once almost completely shattered by a major impact.*

Multiple moons

Until the *Voyager 2* mission, Uranus was known to have five moons: Oberon, Titania, Umbriel, Ariel, and Miranda (all named after characters from English literature). As *Voyager 2* approached, another moon was spotted and named Puck. A further nine small, dark moons also were found. The two innermost moons, Cordelia and Ophelia, on opposite sides of the outer ring, help shepherd the ring particles into line. One astronomer commented that God must have taken a shaker and scattered moons in all directions.

△ *Three of Uranus's main moons are shown here. Oberon (1) has big impact craters, containing dark, carbon-rich material. Ariel (2) is covered in places by small craters and resurfaced in others by eruptions of lava or water. Umbriel (3) has a dark, cratered surface, but no signs of geological activity.*

◁ *The atmosphere of Uranus is made up of hydrogen, helium, and a small percentage of methane. It has very few cloud markings.*

△ *The blue-green gas giant Uranus is four times the size of the Earth. It has a strange magnetic field aligned at 60° to the rotation axis and off-centered 6,200 miles (10,000 km) from the heart of the planet. It may be generated by electrical currents in the watery mantle.*

◁ *Uranus probably has a rocky core with a mantle of ammonia, methane, and water ice that may be partially liquid.*

Strange rotation

Unlike the other planets' axes, Uranus's axis of rotation is at right angles to its orbit around the Sun. So, as *Voyager 2* approached Uranus's south pole, the rings and moons seemed to circle the planet like a target. This also gives Uranus very strange seasons. The poles are the warmest places on the planet. The south pole has a summer lasting 42 years, when the Sun never sets, while the opposite pole is plunged into total darkness for 42 years.

◁ *Uranus rotates at an angle of 97° to the Sun during its 84-year orbit.*

▷ *The orbits of Uranus's five main moons are shown here. From the outside in they are: Oberon, Titania, Umbriel, Ariel, and Miranda. They orbit in circular paths in the same direction as the planet's rotation.*

Neptune

After the discovery of Uranus, astronomers were unable to make sense of its orbit around the Sun—it seemed as if something was pulling it off course. In 1845, Cambridge graduate John Couch Adams suggested this movement was being caused by an eighth planet, and a year later his professor, James Challis, began a search. In France, Urban Leverrier had made similar predictions and, although Challis had seen the new planet without recognizing it, Berlin astronomers used the French predictions to discover Neptune in 1846. They named the blue-green planet after the Roman god of the sea. It is 2.8 billion miles (4.5 billion km) from the Sun and takes 165 years to orbit it (a Neptunian year).

△ *This image, made by Voyager 2 in 1989, has been enhanced to reveal a haze above the atmosphere and white clouds of methane ice.*

◁ *The Great Dark Spot, fringed with methane ice clouds, is as big as the Earth. It travels around Neptune backward. The Solar System's fastest winds blow around it at 1,240 mph (2,000 km/hr).*

△ *Neptune is m[ade] up of a thick ma[ntle] of liquid water [and] gases around a r[ocky] core. It has a m[agnetic] field inclined at [angle to] its axis and 6,20[0 mi.] (10,000 km) off [center]. It has rings ma[de] of large particle[s] and broad band[s of] finer dust.*

Weather forecast

Neptune's atmosphere is 85 percent hydrogen, 13 percent helium, and 2 percent methane. It is bitterly cold (the cloud tops are −346°F [−210°C]), but heat is produced in the interior. Neptune is very active. Clouds of methane rise through the atmosphere and violent winds blow at over 620 mph (1,000 km/hr). One cloud pattern, the Scooter, speeds around the planet passing another feature, the Great Dark Spot, every few days.

△ *The atmosphere is topped by a haze with cirrus clouds of methan[e]. Sunlight causes reactions in the m[ethane] producing hydrocarbon snow. As t[his falls] it reverts to methane gas and rises[.]*

◁ *High-speed winds have stretche[d] these high cirrus clouds of methan[e into] streamers. They cast shadows onto [the] main cloud deck, 30 mi. (50 km) b[elow].*

◁ *Neptune's two main moons, Triton and Nereid, have very different orbits. Nereid's long elliptical orbit lasts 360 days. Triton's 5.9-day orbit circles the planet backward. Both may have been caught by Neptune's gravity as they passed.*

Rings and moons

Before *Voyager 2*'s flyby of Neptune in 1989, only two moons and partial rings were known to astronomers. The craft's cameras confirmed complete rings, bands of dust, and six new moons. The largest is Proteus. It is 271 miles (436 km) across and has a giant 93-mile (150-km) crater. Then comes Larissa at 129 miles (208 km). The other four moons lie between the rings. The outermost moon, Nereid, may be a captured comet. Neptune's largest moon, Triton, is 1,681 miles (2,706 km) across. With no high mountains and few craters, its surface may have been flooded by eruptions of liquid water and ammonia. Most of its surface is ice, but the poles are capped with a pink snow of frozen nitrogen.

▽ *Triton's south pole is capped by a light, pinkish substance that is probably frozen nitrogen accumulated during its long winter in shadow. The grooved and wrinkled surface to the north has a red tint, possibly due to hydrocarbons produced by the action of sunlight.*

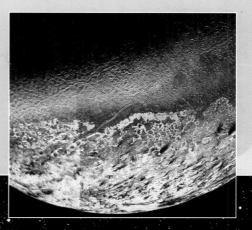

...s imagined view from the surface of Triton shows Neptune ... horizon and an active nitrogen geyser erupting from the ...e. Pressure keeps nitrogen liquid deep below the ground.

As it rises, it explodes as ice crystals and vapor. The eruption carries this 18.5 miles (30 km) high, before it blows away in the thin wind, raining a dark streak of dust down onto the surface.

Pluto

In order to explain the orbit of Uranus, astronomers realized they had to discover something else. An American astronomer, Percival Lowell, predicted a planet larger than Earth and searched for it in vain. (Pluto appeared on his photographs, but he failed to recognize it.) However, Clyde Tombaugh, a successor at the observatory Lowell founded in Arizona, painstakingly compared star after star and finally found one that moved. Named Pluto (Greek god of the underworld) at the suggestion of an 11-year-old girl, it is 3.7 billion miles (6 billion km) from the Sun and one four-hundredth the mass of Earth.

△ *This image of Pluto is made up from measurements taken by the* Hubble Space Telescope. *The lightest patches may be nitrogen ice.*

△ *Even the most powerful Earth-based telescopes can only just make out the faint disk of Pluto. No probe has visited Pluto, and it will be many years before one will be able to fill in the details.*

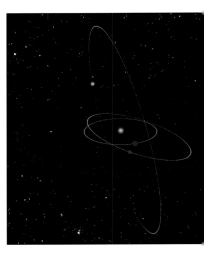

△ *Pluto is usually the farthest plan from the Sun, but its elliptical orbit* (orange) *briefly brings it closer tha Neptune* (blue). *Some astronomers predict that a Planet X* (green) *follo a steeply inclined orbit far outside F The Kuiper Belt—a ring of small, icy objects—lies beyond the planets*

▽ *Icy Pluto hangs just above th horizon in this imagined view its moon, Charon. The Sun bright star in the sky to the Charon is half the size of F and twenty times closer th the Moon is to the Earth. permanently frozen surfac have a solidified sea of met*

eing double

en it was first discovered, Pluto's mass and density were unknown,
no one knew if it was the final explanation for the outer planets'
its. If Pluto had a moon, however, the masses could be calculated
m that moon's orbit. There the matter rested until 1978, when James
risty was trying to make precise measurements of Pluto at the U.S.
val Observatory. At first, his picture seemed pear shaped. Suddenly,
realized he was seeing not one object, but two. He named the second
moon Charon for his wife, and also
for the mythological ferryman to
the ancient Greek underworld.

▷ *Both Pluto and Charon are denser than the other outer planets and their moons. They must have big, rocky cores covered by thick layers of water ice, frozen methane, and nitrogen.*

his picture shows Pluto and ron. Pluto at 1,400 miles 0 km) across is far smaller our Moon, while Charon is less 750 miles (1,200 km) across.

◁ *A faint line among the points of stars reveals an object in the Kuiper Belt. Only a few miles*
oss, *a few hundred of these* ects *have been observed with* verful *infrared telescopes.*

Planet X and beyond

Pluto, however, did not account for all the
discrepancies in Uranus's orbit, and astronomers
started searching for a tenth planet, Planet X.
Clyde Tombaugh searched for 13 years, plotting
the positions of 45 million stars and identifying
775 asteroids in the process. Some people predicted
that a planet would be found in an orbit angled to
the other planets, while others thought that the
Sun had a distant, dark companion. There may
also be billions of comets beyond the planets
adding their gravitational effect. A belt of
icy objects known as the Kuiper Belt has been
discovered far beyond Pluto. Each object
is only a few miles across, and they may be the
frozen leftovers from planetary formation.

△ *Pluto has a thin atmosphere of nitrogen and methane. It thickens as the planet warms slightly, when its elliptical orbit brings it nearer the Sun. Polar caps of methane ice may be deposited as Pluto cools again.*

Comets

Comets are among the most beautiful and exciting sights in the sky. They are made all the more mysterious by their unpredictability, leading people in the past to think that they were omens of either good or evil. Five hundred years ago, they were thought to be part of the atmosphere. Then, in 1577, Danish astronomer Tycho Brahe figured out the distance to a comet and showed that they came from beyond the planets and rounded the Sun before returning to deep space. We now know that there must be a vast number of comets in the outer regions of the Solar System, far beyond the planets. In fact, there could be billions waiting in the deep freeze of space.

△ *This engraving from the* Nuremberg Chronicle *(published in 1493) depicts the sighting of Halley's Comet in A.D. 684.*

△ *In the* Adoration of the Magi *by Giotto, Halley's Comet is shown as the star of Bethlehem, above the stable.*

△ *This computer simulation shows how the front dust shield of* Giotto *looked after speeding past the nucleus of Halley's Comet. Dust particles punched holes in the metal.* Giotto *took a close-up picture of the comet's dark nucleus* (right) *silhouetted against brighter jets of gas.*

Halley's Comet

Edmond Halley studied the records of comets and realized that the comets of 1531, 1607, and 1682 were actually the same object. He predicted correctly this comet's return in 1759, although he never lived to see it. In fact, Halley's Comet has been seen 30 times since 240 B.C. It is depicted in the Bayeux Tapestry, which shows the Norman Conquest of England in 1066, and in a painting of the Nativity by the Italian artist Giotto, based on his sighting of the comet in 1301. In 1986, a probe named *Giotto* visited Halley's Comet.

▽ *In 1997, Comet Hale-Bopp gave a great display. Its nucleus was unusually large and it started to brighten beyond Jupiter's orbit.*

△ *This image of Comet Hale-Bopp, taken in 1996, is colored to show the bright coma as well as the dark nucleus embedded deep within it.*

The core of a comet

Comets are all show and little substance. At the center is a small nucleus, only a few miles across, like a dirty snowball. It may contain lumps of [rock], but they are loosely bound by ice, so comets often break up. As the nucleus approaches the inner [Solar] System, the ice begins to vaporize, creating the bright coma (a sphere of gas and dust around the nucleus) and tail, which can be millions of miles long. A crust of black, carbon-rich material covers the surface with jets of gas breaking out through cracks. Each time a comet passes the Sun it loses millions of tons of ice, eventually leaving a dead, dark nucleus or just a trail of dust.

...e nucleus of a comet is like a ...dirty snowball. Jets of gas and ...scape through fissures in its black, ...tlike surface, blown by the solar ...to form a tail. Here, the surface has ...ut away to reveal the icy interior, ...nding a loosely bound, rocky core.

△ *Comets have two tails. Electrically charged ions of gas always point directly away from the Sun. The yellower dust tail lags slightly and curves with the comet's motion.*

Dead comets and shooting stars

Long after a comet has run out of bright gas and faded for good, anything that is left of the nucleus, along with a stream of dusty particles, continues in the same orbit. When the Earth passes through this orbit, thousands of the particles burn up as shooting stars in the atmosphere. These are the meteor showers that seem to radiate out from the same place in the sky at the same time each year. Spectacular storms look as if they emerge from particular constellations. For example, the Perseid shower, which follows Comet Swift-Tuttle, appears from the constellation Perseus, while the Orionids, which follow Halley's Comet, seem to come from Orion.

△ *Blown back by the solar wind (a constant stream of electrically charged particles emitted by the Sun), a comet's tails always point away from the Sun. The tails are longest closest to the Sun, when gas production is at its highest.*

Oort Cloud

...ut, on the edge of the Solar System, lies a gigantic ... of billions of frozen comets called the Oort Cloud. ...e comets are concentrated in a disk beyond the orbit ...uto, while others are randomly distributed up to a ...year or more away. The gravity of nearby stars ...cks" these comets from their orbits so that they fall ...rd the Sun. About ten comets a year are newcomers ...e inner Solar System, where many become trapped. ...Oort Cloud may be debris left over from when the ...System formed. If so, comets may be able to tell ...at conditions were like when the Sun was born.

△ *An exposure of only a few seconds captured the bright streaks of the Leonid meteor shower, which seems to radiate from the constellation Leo and follows Comet Tempel-Tuttle.*

◁ The Sun has been burning for ab[out] five billion years. Like all stars, it is [a] huge ball of very hot gas. Its consta[nt] stream of sunshine keeps our planet warm, enables plants to photosynth[esize] and ultimately sustains all life.

▽ During a total eclipse, the corona—the outer layer of t[he] Sun's atmosphere—becomes visible. It [can] reach temperature[s] of up to 3,600,000°[F] (2,000,000°C).

The Active Sun

△ Sunlight scatters off dust and clouds in Earth's atmosphere to produce spectacular sunrises and sunsets.

The Sun is our nearest star, the center of the Solar System, and the source, directly or indirectly, of almost all the energy we use. The Sun is extremely hot—about 10,800°F (6,000°C) at the surface, or photosphere, and 27,000,000°F (15,000,000°C) at the core. The core temperature and pressure are high enough for an energy-generating process called nuclear fusion to take place. Protons, the nuclei of hydrogen atoms, fuse together to make deuterium or heavy hydrogen, then helium. At each stage, mass is lost in the form of energy. Altogether the Sun loses 4 million tons of mass every second, which is converted into the 400 quintillion megawatts of energy it needs to support itself and to shine. Most of the energy radiates as heat, light, and gamma rays, taking thousands of years to reach the surface. But some escapes straight through the Sun, carried by ghostly particles called neutrinos, produced in the nuclear reactions.

This x-ray image of the Sun and its corona was recorded by the Japanese satellite Yohkoh in 1992. The brightest and hottest [areas] occur above sunspots, where hot gases flare up.

▷ Nuclear reactions take place inside the Sun's core, and the energy slowly radiates out to a distance of about 370,000 miles (600,000 km). Huge bubbles of hot gas continue the transfer of energy to the surface.

Observing the Sun

You should not look at the Sun directly, and certainly never through a telescope or binoculars—you risk being blinded for life. It is possible, however, to project an image onto a sheet of paper using binoculars, a lens, or even a pinhole in a sheet of cardboard. This is essentially what solar astronomers do, focusing the light down long tubes, through filters, and onto an observation table.

Unobstructed view

The Sun is best viewed from beyond our turbulent atmosphere. From space, the Sun can be seen in other wavelengths such as x rays, revealing the superhot flares that leap from the surface. Several spacecraft have studied the Sun directly, including *Skylab* in the 1970s and *SolarMax* in the 1980s. *Ulysses* has left the plane of the planets to study the magnetic field and solar wind above the poles of the Sun. And Europe's *SOHO* hangs between Earth and the Sun looking at sunquakes and flares and spotting storms of particles on their way to Earth.

[Eclipse!]

[Abou]t once a year, the Moon comes between the Sun [and E]arth, casting a shadow. When the Moon is close [enou]gh to Earth in its orbit, it masks the Sun's disk [complete]ly, causing a total eclipse.

[Du]ring a total eclipse, part of the [Earth] is plunged into darkness. People [in the] outer shadow see a partial eclipse.

△ The Sun is ringing like a bell. Scientists can record the vibrations by seeing how the movement stretches or compresses light from different regions. The sound waves are created in the solar convective zone, or the outer layer of the Sun.

△ The McMath Solar Telescope in Arizona focuses the Sun's image down a 499-foot (152-m) diagonal tube to instruments below.

Outside the Sun

The hot, electrically charged gas within the Sun generates very powerful magnetic fields. Where these break the surface, huge jets or loops of hot gas called prominences lift off into space. Dark, relatively cool patches on the Sun's surface are called sunspots. These form in pairs or groups, and represent points where the magnetic field lines leave and rejoin the surface. Rapid eruptions called solar flares also arise along these lines. They usually last no longer than ten minutes, and release the energy equivalent of a million hydrogen bombs. Together with the solar wind (a constant stream of charged particles flowing from the Sun), they create a vast envelope, known as the heliosphere, around the Solar System.

△ *A visible light image of the Sun, taken using the McMath Solar Telescope in Arizona. Several sunspots can clearly be seen on the photosphere, or the visible surface of the Sun.*

△ *Prominences of hot gas break free from the Sun's surface and leap out hundreds of thousands of miles into space.*

△ *The Sun broadcasts strong radio signals that were first noticed in the 1940s. The brightest areas in this radio image occur where gas flares off into space above pairs of sunspots.*

△ *This false-color photograph shows a group of sunspots. The spots form in pairs with opposite magnetic poles. The dark centers of the spots are the coolest, lowest regions where strong magnetic fields slow the upward flow of heat. Around them, bubbles of gas rise, cool, and move away.*

changing Sun

Sun is not as constant as it appears. By tracking ots, it is clear that it rotates at the equator once 25 days, and at the poles once every 35 days. This rence results in magnetic field lines getting wrapped d the Sun until they break through the surface at ots. The pattern of sunspots changes in a cycle of 11 years. At the start of the cycle, spots begin to r near the poles. As they fade, spots appear nearer and nearer to the equator, where they cause a peak of solar activity.

◁ *Magnetic field lines snake out from a sunspot with north polarity and reenter a spot with south polarity. The magnetic lines form tubes along which hot gas flows.*

S

Solar weather

There are less dramatic changes, too. Between 1645 and 1715, there were virtually no sunspots. This period coincided with extreme winters in Europe, and sometimes is known as the "Little Ice Age." Evidence from other Sunlike stars suggests that, for up to 20 percent of their time, they have no sunspots.

◁ *These loops of hot gas were photographed in ultraviolet by Skylab in 1973. Great loops arch up between pairs of sunspots and can remain relatively stable for many hours or even days.*

The end of the Sun

It probably took the Sun 3.5 billion years to reach its present brightness, during which time plants were slowly using up carbon dioxide from Earth's atmosphere, reducing the greenhouse effect and keeping our climate roughly constant. The Sun probably will continue to shine at its present level for another two billion years. But in about six billion years' time, hydrogen will begin to run out at the core, and the Sun will begin to expand rapidly and cool as it becomes a dying star called a red giant. This will engulf the inner planets, including Earth.

△ *In about six billion years' time, Earth's atmosphere and oceans will boil away as the dying Sun becomes a red giant. As this giant star expands, the baked husk of our planet will be swallowed up and become part of a new generation of stars and planets.*

▽ Swirling nebulae of dust and gas are the nurseries of stars. Often, they are themselves the ashes of earlier generations, cooked and spewed out from short-lived, massive stars.

Star Birth

△ Knots form in the gas as gravity pulls it together. As t.. compresses, it begins to heat u..

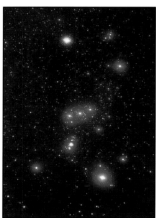

△ Below the line of three stars that form the belt of Orion is Orion's Sword. At its center lies the distinctive Orion Nebula, a birthplace of stars.

The backdrop of stars used to be thought of as constant and unchanging. Over human lifetimes, there is little detectable change; but over the billi.. of years of galactic life, stars are born, live their lives, grow old, and die. Spac.. by human standards, appears very, very empty. But collect together all the gas dust of supposedly empty space, and there is more matter than all the stars an.. planets put together. It is out of these thin clouds, or nebulae, that new stars a.. born. Over 12 billion years ago, when the Universe itself was young, clouds of hydrogen and helium created the first stars to ever shine. Now, all kinds of other elements are mixed in, the ashes of earlier generations of stars. These combine to make the stars we see forming in dusty nebulae today.

Conception!

Stars tend to be born not singly but in nurseries, where sufficiently dense clouds of gas have accumulated. Star formation can be triggered simply by the gravitational pull of the gas, or when a shock wave passes through it from, for example, a nearby exploding star or intergalactic collision.

▷ Altogether, 700 young stars have been spotted in the dust and gas clouds of the Orion Nebula, illuminated here by visible and ultraviolet light.

◁ An infrare.. image (left) of t.. Orion Nebula take.. by the Hubble Space Telescope reveals that .. young stars lie inside the tee.. mass of gas and dust (above)

△ *...e gas begins to spiral in ... The protostar expels ... gas from its poles.*

△ *Nuclear fusion begins in the hot core. Gas is expelled in a wind that blows the dust away.*

△ *Finally, the star begins to shine steadily.*

Getting warm

As knots of gas inside the cloud become compressed, they begin to warm up. As it contracts, the cloud rotates faster, making the gas form into a disk. Matter falling inward from the disk is ejected in jets from the poles. Eventually, the central protostar becomes so hot and compressed that the process of nuclear fusion begins at its core. This in turn causes more material to be blown off and, finally, the remains of the disk blow away—apart from any lumps that are forming into planets—and the new star shines into clear space.

Seeing cool, seeing deep

At the different stages of a star's birth and life cycle, matter glows with different wavelengths. When stars begin to form, warm gas radiates in the infrared wavelength, while cooler dust and molecules glow at the submillimeter radio wavelengths. Infrared and radio waves can also penetrate the thick clouds, so it is at these wavelengths that astronomers peer into the nebulae and watch stars being born.

...y stars hatch from EGGs (Evaporating Gaseous Globules), ...gerlike tips emerging from this pillar of gas in the Eagle ...a. This picture was taken by the Hubble Space Telescope.

...e Hubble Space Telescope *has revealed more than 150 of these ...e knots in the Orion Nebula. They provide the best evidence ...that planetary systems can form at the same time as stars.*

Star Life

△ *As Earth moves in its orbit around the Sun, nearby stars appear to move against the distant background. This displacement is called "parallax," and it is used to measure the distances to stars.*

Stars come in all sizes and colors. Look up on a clear, dark night and you will see hundreds, perhaps thousands of sta Look with a powerful telescope and you will see millions, or e billions. Some are bright, others faint. Some look blue, others yellow, or red. There are stars that are bright simply because th are nearby. Certain stars are, in absolute terms, hundreds of ti brighter than the Sun; others are thousands of times dimmer. star's color reflects its surface temperature. Blue stars are very while red ones are cooler. Their ages vary as well. Some are al as old as the Universe; others are babies in comparison. It is the little ones that live longest. Big stars burn up their nuclea fuel much faster and only last a few million years.

The main sequence

This is a fixed relationship between the temperature and brightness of most stars. They begin as red dwarfs and become hotter and brighter. The period of a star's life when it is shining almost constantly is known as the "main sequence." How long this lasts depends on the star's mass. When the hydrogen burning in its core runs out, the star expands and cools into a red giant, leaving the main sequence. Eventually, the star sheds its outer layers, leaving a slowly cooling white dwarf.

▷ Hipparcos, *the European satellite, has measured the precise position of more than 120,000 stars. It found that some are closer than we previously thought.*

△ *The Pleiades open cluster of stars is sometimes known as the Seven Sisters, after the seven stars clearly visible to the naked eye. This cluster contains, in fact, almost 500 young, blue stars.*

How far to the stars

The brightest star in the sky, Sirius, is close (8.6 light years), and, although it is in reality 26 times brighter than the Sun, it is not nearly as bright as some more distant stars. To find out how bright a star really is, yc need to know how far away it is. The first step in figu out the distance of a star is to measure its position. By doing this twice, six months apart, when the Earth is opposite sides of the Sun, a nearby star's distance can calculated by using parallax. Move your head from si side. Objects close to you seem to move against the me distant background. Earth's orbit is equivalent to mov your head; and the apparent motion of stars against th distant background gives a measure of distance.

nse of scale

listance to the stars is vast. Proxima Centuri, the
st, is 25,000,000,000,000 miles (40,000,000,000,000
way, while others are hundreds of times farther out.
ly, miles are not very convenient units of measure. So,
nomers use light years—a measurement of distance,
me. One light year is the distance light travels in one
Proxima Centuri is 4.2 light years away.

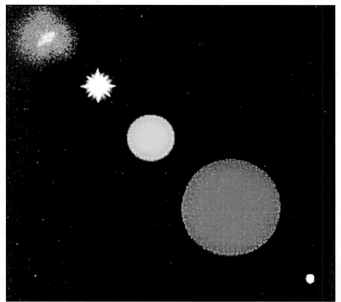

△ *The life story of a star like the Sun begins in a cloud
of gas from which a bright, young protostar condenses.
For eight billion years it shines as a yellow star, then
expands into a red giant before becoming a white dwarf.*

Variable stars

Some stars appear to vary in their brightness, either
erratically, or in a regular cycle. Sometimes it is because
they are in binary pairs and one eclipses the other.
Young and unstable stars flare out great masses of hot
gas into space, while old, red supergiants send out black,
sooty clouds of carbon. Others pulsate regularly. One
type, the so-called Cepheid variables, alternately inflates
and contracts, brightening and fading at a rate directly
related to its overall brightness. This makes these stars
useful for measuring distances in the Universe.

*us (top) in the constellation Canis Major is the brightest
the sky. Sometimes known as the Dog Star, it is part of
ry pair. Its companion star is a faint white dwarf.*

and clusters

un shines alone in space, but most stars are members
oups. Frequently, they are in pairs known as binaries.
are in less stable groups of three, or in double
ies of four. Stars turn up in larger groups, too, such as
leiades. Some of the most closely packed groups of
called globular clusters, may contain millions
rs, light months rather than light years apart.

▷ *This globular cluster
in our neighboring
galaxy, Andromeda,
has at least 300,000
stars. From the amount
of helium that has built
up, astronomers have
estimated that the stars
are almost as old as
the Universe itself.*

Star Death

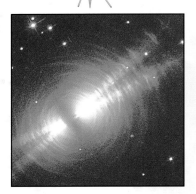

△ *The Egg Nebula consists of concentric shells of gas ejected by a red giant star near the end of its life. The "searchlights" are areas where light and jets of particles penetrate gaps in the swirling clouds of dust.*

Stars the size of our Sun swell up as hydrogen runs low in their core and they shed layers of gas to form what are known as planetary nebulae. Left behind at the center is a white dwarf star, which slowly cools to a cinder over billions of years. Bigger stars live more brief and violent lives. Within them, a constant battle rages between the pressure of the heat holding them up and the crushing force of gravity. If a star's mass is over 40 percent greater than the Sun's mass, not even electrons can hold it up when its nuclear fuel runs out. Electrons in the core are squashed so hard that they fuse with protons to make neutrons. The resulting matter has a density of 4.8 billion tons per cubic inch and forms a star no bigger than a city, but weighing more than the Sun. The energy released as the core collapses tears through the outer layers of the dying star in a huge supernova explosion.

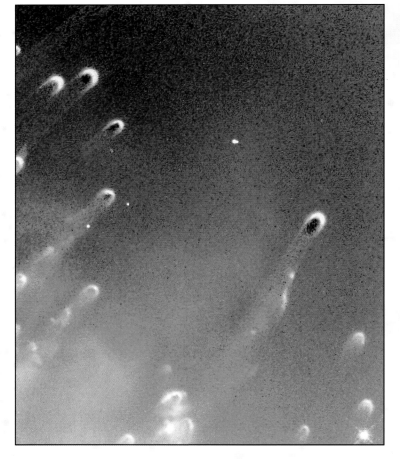

△ *Tadpolelike knots of material in the Helix Planetary Nebula plow into gases ejected earlier from a dying star. Each knot is larger than our own Solar System.*

▷ *This picture was taken by* the Hubble Space Telescope *ten years after the explosion of supernova 1987a. The remains of the star lie in the center. A blast wave moves toward a ring of matter shed by the giant star 30,000 years before it exploded. The blast is just reaching the ring, causing it to brighten* (indicated by arrow).

Going supernova

On February 23, 1987, Canadian astronomer Ian Shel was making routine observations using a telescope in Chile when he noticed a very bright star that he did not remember seeing before. He soon realized that he had spotted an exploding star—a supernova lying 17(light years away. A few hours earlier, special undergr detectors in the United States and Japan had picked a pulse of ghostly *neutrinos*, particles created when th iron core of a giant star collapses and a neutron star fo The process had caused a tremendous explosion that the star apart in a blaze of hot new radioactive eleme

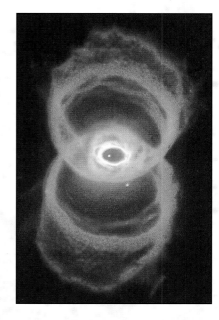

◁ *When the star NGC 7027 swelled into a red giant, it started to shed gas and formed the blue, spherical shell. As the process became more violent, it produced the red and yellow material.*

▷ *The Hourglass Nebula has formed around a star reaching the end of its life. A stellar wind has blown out from the poles creating the double ring.*

◁ *The Crab Nebula is the remnant of a star that exploded in A.D. 1054. At its center is a tiny, superdense neutron star, pulsing as it spins thirty times a second and ejecting particles that interact with the gas.*

The stars, our ancestors

The first matter in the Universe was almost all helium and hydrogen. All the other elements around us today, including carbon, silicon, oxygen, and nitrogen, were cooked up in the nuclear furnaces of stars, scattered into space, and reformed into solar systems such as ours. All elements that are heavier than iron were created and spewed out in supernova explosions. Our world and even our bodies are made, quite literally, of stardust.

rs

year, several supernova explosions are spotted in
t galaxies, and there is plenty of evidence for past
ions nearer home. In A.D. 1054, Chinese astronomers
ed a bright new star, or nova, in the direction of the
llation of Taurus. Today, it is still visible as the Crab
a, a bright, expanding shell of radioactive gas and
. At its center is a small white star sending out radio
s thirty times a second. When it was discovered in
it was given the name LGM1 (L for little, G for
and M for man). This is not an alien distress beacon.
pulsar—an ultradense neutron star, flashing a beam
iation as it spins. Hundreds have been found since,
spinning up to a thousand times per second.

△ *The bright ray of a pulsar sweeps across space as a neutron star spins on its axis. Escaping electrons are funneled by the intense magnetic field, which emits radiation and light.*

⊲ *"Oh my ears and whiskers, how late it's getting!"* *At least both Alice and the White Rabbit agree what time it is, as Alice sets out on a journey into a black hole.*

Black Hole!

While some dying stars turn into superdense neutron stars, others collapse even further. In a star that is more than three times the Sun's mass, gravity violently crushes matter inward. It continues to collapse before disappearing into an incredibly dense but dimensionless point called a singularity. A black hole is the space around a singularity, and nothing that falls in can ever go fast enough to escape—not even light. Black holes vary in size—the bigger the singularity, the wider the black hole.

Time for a change

A black hole plays strange tricks on the fabric of space and time, curving it in on itself. If you were able to watch someone falling toward a black hole's outer edge, or event horizon, you would see their watch ticking slower and slower. At the same time, they would become redder and redder, until they faded from view.

△ *Gas is dragged off a massive star* (above right), *and spirals violently into a black hole. The spinning disk heats up until it emits x rays, and a jet of hot matter shoots from the poles.*

The long stretch

If you were the unfortunate person falling into a black hole, your watch would seem to tick normally and you would remain your usual color. But you would have other things to worry about. The gravity would pull so hard that it would stretch you out like spaghetti. Your remains would rapidly spiral in, like water down a cosmic drain, and friction would

Alice gets close to the black
...ts gravity begins to act more
...feet than her head and she
...to stretch. It also stretches the
...and her feet grow redder.
...notices no change in the rate
...atch ticks, but already the
...t sees her watch running slow.

▷ *The gravitational well
of a black hole or even a
massive star distorts the
fabric of space-time. A ray
of light traveling from a
star to Earth is bent as
it shines past, changing the
apparent position of the star.*

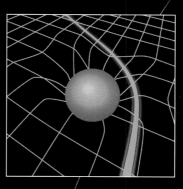

Hunting the invisible

Although astronomers cannot see black holes directly, they can
detect them through their effects. Stars often come in pairs, and
if one of the pair has collapsed into a black hole it may also
pull in gas from the companion star. As the gas spirals
in, it emits x rays. By looking at these x-ray sources,
astronomers can study the invisible black hole.

▽ *In what to Alice are the next few seconds, she will be beyond the
point of no return—the event
horizon. Meanwhile, the Rabbit
is getting later and later.*

...Alice really has
...s. She becomes "spaghettified"
...ravitational forces begin to pull her
...Compared to the Rabbit's watch,
...e is running slower and slower.

great escape

...ugh you could never escape from a black
...something does emerge from them. Pairs of
...les, created on the event horizon itself, end up
...one falling in, one coming out. The loss of
...y is known as "Hawking radiation." It is so faint,
...ver, that it would take 100 billion billion billion
...n billion billion years for a black hole with
...ass of our Sun to evaporate.

The Milky Way

We have seen how ideas have changed from the ancient notion of our Earth as the center of the Universe to one where the Sun rules the planets. Today, we know that the Sun is just one among about 200 billion stars in the great star city of our galaxy, the Milky Way. The whole galaxy is like a vast disk with a bulge in the middle (somewhat like two fried eggs, put back to back), with great spiral arms of stars. About three-quarters of the way out along the Orion Arm is our local star, the Sun. The Milky Way is about 100,000 light years across (the Solar System is only about 12 light hours across) and rotates in space, spinning fastest at its center.

△ *This fish-eye view of the entire night sky above Australia is dominated by the billions of stars that make up the Milky Way.*

Highway of stars

Look up at the sky on a clear, dark night, away from city lights, and you can see the great highway of stars that is the Milky Way. It is most dense toward its center, in the constellation of Sagittarius. You will see nearby bright stars, clusters of stars, and a faint haze of millions of distant stars. The darker patches that look like holes are really huge clouds of dust. The faint remains of ancient supernova explosions show up as a wispy structure of gas all around us.

△ *This near-infrared view of the Milky Way clearly shows the central bulge of the galaxy from our position within it.*

Among the crowd

We cannot see the center of the galaxy (it is shrouded in gas and dust), but infrared and radio waves can penetrate the clouds, giving hints of violent processes at work. It is a very crowded place, with millions of stars and immense quantities of gas. There is a barlike structure, and clouds of molecules. Strong magnetic fields have drawn gas out into thin filaments, and a fountain of antimatter rises thousands of light years from the galactic plane.

CYGNUS ARM

PERSEUS ARM

CENTRAL BULGE

ORION ARM

SAGITTARIUS ARM   CRUX-CENTAURUS ARM

◁ The Milky Way has a complex structure of spiral arms and a densely packed central bulge of older stars. Some of the main features can be seen above. The Sun is in the Orion arm.

△ Infrared images can see through the clouds of dust and give a tantalizing glimpse of the Milky Way's center, where a black hole may lurk.

Shifting heart

Three hundred light years from the galaxy's core lies a gamma-ray source called the Great Annihilator. Once thought to be the center of the Milky Way, it produces jets of antimatter and emits gamma rays. It is probably a black hole. The true center is now known to be Sagittarius A*. This may be a monster black hole more than a million times the mass of the Sun. But if it is, the beast at the center of the galaxy appears to be sleeping right now.

△ The 28-inch (73-cm) wavelength radio map (1) reveals high-velocity electrons moving in a magnetic field. It helps astronomers to plot the magnetic field of the galaxy. The infrared map (2) is especially bright where there are dust clouds warmed by hot new stars. The blue "S" is dust in our Solar System. The 8-inch (21-cm) radio map (3) reveals atomic hydrogen in gas clouds between stars. The gas emits a very precise frequency, helping scientists to trace its motion in the rotating galaxy.

Our Local Group

The Milky Way and the Andromeda galaxies are immense spirals of stars, island universes in their own right. They are the two largest and most important members of the Local Group, a cluster of galaxies stretching five million light years across space. The Local Group contains some 30 galaxies, loosely bound together in each other's gravitational pull. Andromeda, which has twice as many stars as our own galaxy, is located near another small spiral. The other members of the group are even smaller, and are either irregular blobs of stars, like the Magellanic clouds near our own spiral galaxy, or even dwarf galaxies.

Cannibal galaxies

It appears that over billions of years, the big spirals, including our own Milky Way, have grown by eating up their neighbors. Some of the nearby dwarf galaxies will be gobbled up by our galaxy in a few million years' time. And even the great spiral Andromeda Galaxy itself is coming toward our own galaxy at about 186 miles (300 km) every second. It still has a long way to go, but eventually the two galaxies may pass through one another, or even merge. The distances between stars are so immense that few will collide, but great clouds of gas and dust might be stirred up into star formation.

▽ In 1912, the American astronomer Henrietta Leavitt discovered that stars called Cepheid variables change their brightness in a predictable way.

▽ The Virgo cluster conta_ than 1,000 galaxies. Virgo 50 million light years awa_ is the center of our supercl_

△ Henrietta Leavitt

△ Virgo cluster

△ Cepheid star (center)

△ Cepheid star (cen_

△ The changing brightness of a Cepheid variable star, see_ here on the left at its most dim, and on the right at its brigh_ allows astronomers to measure the distance to the galaxie_ After the discovery of this type of star, the painstaking mapping of the Universe, galaxy by galaxy, could begin.

△ The Local Group consists of about 30 galaxies. Our own spiral galaxy, the Milky Way, is surrounded by dwarf galaxies and a few irregular galaxies. To the right is the great Andromeda Galaxy and its smaller companions, including the spiral M33. The other irregular galaxies are more isolated.

TYPE OF GAL_

Dwarf gala_

Irregular gal_

Spiral galaxy

...tz Zwicky discovered that
...es are grouped in clusters,
...f them thousands strong
...illions of light years across.

▽ *The* Hubble Space Telescope *revealed
that the core of the Andromeda Galaxy has
a double nucleus. This may have resulted
from a merger with another galaxy.*

◁ *The Andromeda Galaxy has a
spiral form similar to the Milky Way.
Andromeda is 2.2 million light years
away, and 150,000 light years across.*

Rotating galaxies

The spiral shape of many galaxies gives
the impression that they are rotating.
However, it is not the stars that are
going around and around, but the arms,
with the stars passing through them.
The arms rotate over hundreds of
millions of years, their outside ends
trailing behind the faster inner regions.
In our own galaxy, it takes the Sun over
200 million years to complete an orbit
and come back to the same position.
This period is sometimes called
the cosmic year.

Superclusters

Even the vast Local Group is a small
backyard on the intergalactic scale.
We are part of a much larger grouping
of other clusters, which together form
the Local Supercluster. Our Local
Group is being pulled by gravity
toward the Virgo cluster, the center
of the Local Supercluster (also known
as the Virgo Supercluster), at a speed
of 168 miles (270 km) per second.
Superclusters are among the largest
structures seen in the Universe, but
even the Local Supercluster is just
one of many others stretching
billions of light years
across the Universe.

△ *Andromeda Galaxy*

△ *Andromeda's core*

ANDROMEDA

M33

△ *Fritz Zwicky*

KY

Expanding Universe

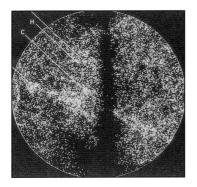

△ *The dark, vertical band in this map of galaxies is where our own galaxy, the Milky Way, blocks the view. We are moving at 373 miles (600 km) per second toward the Great Attractor, the dense, bright cluster near the center.*

The speed of galaxies is one of the easier things to calculate in the Universe. The light from stars and galaxies comes with a very convenient measure. If a galaxy is moving away from us, the wavelength of its light is stretched, or redshifted. If it is coming toward us, the wavelength gets squashed and shifted toward the blue end of the spectrum. In 1929, Edwin Hubble discovered that the more distant a galaxy is, the more its light is redshifted. And it soon became clear that the farther a galaxy is from our own, the faster it is speeding away. Hubble concluded that the reason for this is not that our galaxy is at the center of the Universe, but rather that the entire Universe is expanding. If this is so, then there must have been a time when all the galaxies were much closer together.

Mapping the Universe

By using redshift to measure the distances to galaxies, astronomers have begun to map the Universe in three dimensions. It is an enormous task but already some very large structures have been revealed. Some areas are like voids or bubbles with very few galaxies in them. Around them are slabs and filaments rich in galaxies. One particular structure forms what has been called the Great Wall, and is at least a billion light years across. There might be a repeating structure of such walls, a bit like a picket fence, with walls about 400 million light years apart.

▽ *On the largest scale, the Universe is like a vast foam, with superclusters and walls of galaxies located along the boundaries of giant bubbles, or voids in space.*

△ *If a galaxy or star is moving toward us, the wave in its light become squashed together, or blueshifted, so it looks more blue. If, on the ot hand, the object is receding from us, the light becomes stretched, or redshifted.*

◁ *This slice through the Universe shows all the galaxies that have had their redshifts measured. Faint structures are visible. Black areas have not yet been fully surveyed.*

▽ *The* 2DF *instrument on the Anglo-Australian Telescope can measure the redshifts of up to 400 galaxies at once.*

The Great Attractor

The Universe does not expand evenly in every direction. Huge concentrations of galaxies put a gravitational brake on the process. Whole streams of galaxies end up resisting the expansion—we are part of such a stream. Beyond the great Virgo supercluster, there appears to be something pulling us and thousands of other galaxies toward it. It has been called the Great Attractor, and it lies in the approximate direction of the constellation Perseus. It acts as if it has a mass of 50 million billion suns, equivalent to hundreds of thousands of galaxies. At one time it was thought that it might be a monster black hole or some other strange object. Now it is generally believed to be an irregularity, or a knot, in the clouds of galaxies. Even so, it has enough gravity to pull our whole local group of galaxies toward it at a velocity of about 373 miles (600 km) per second.

is image of the Andromeda Galaxy has color coded to show the redshift and hift caused by the galaxy's rotation.

The Galactic Zoo

△ *Some galaxies, such as NGC 1300, appear to lose their tightly wound spiral structure as they evolve and develop a broad bar.*

The Universe contains around 100 billion galaxies, and each galaxy, on average, is made up of about 100 billion stars. Galaxies come in many different shapes and sizes. Spiral galaxies can be tightly wound or loose, while others have a broad bar across their center. Some galaxies have no obvious shape, and are classed as irregular. The largest of all galaxies are elliptical. Stars are no longer forming in elliptical galaxies. It could be that most galaxies begin as spirals but, as they interact with one another, all their gas is pulled into the stars. The spiral structure disappears and becomes an elliptical galaxy.

Looking back in time

The most distant galaxies ever seen are probably more than ten billion light years away. This means that light has taken ten billion years to reach us so what we are seeing is the light that left them when the Universe was ten billion years younger. By peering back across such distances, it is possible to see galaxies as they form. In one particular study by the *Hubble Space Telescope*, no fewer than 18 dwarf galaxies were spotted moving together under the influence of each other's gravity. This suggests that galaxies are formed when much smaller galaxies merge. The final stages of this process can be seen today in our own galaxy as it swallows up a few remaining dwarf galaxies.

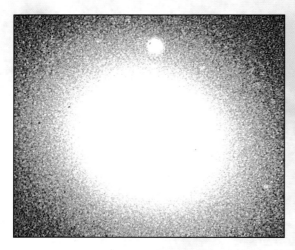

▷ *Astronomers believe that these faint smudges of star cluster, 11 billion light years away, are the building blocks that will merge to form the core of a new galaxy.*

◁ *Giant elliptical galaxies, such as M49, are the final stage in galactic evolution. They contain almost no young stars.*

△ *The central hub of M51, or the Whirlpool Galaxy, is mostly made up of old, yellow sta spiral arms contain young, blue stars, while of gas and dust connects it to a second galax*

2 is a spiral galaxy, seen here from the
The disturbance at the center is probably
by the galaxy plowing into a gas cloud.

Starburst

There must have been a time when the first stars started to shine, a spectacular period in the history of the Universe, which had been dark since the Big Bang of creation. When astronomers peer through the great clouds of dust in which stars are made, they can see whole galaxies shining brightly with the sudden birth of millions of big, hot stars. More recent starburst galaxies are also seen where galaxies have smashed into one another, stirring up the dust lanes and triggering a new burst of star formation. In one of these, called Arp 220, the rate of star formation is probably a hundred times that of our entire Milky Way Galaxy, but concentrated into a nucleus a hundred times smaller.

◁ *Arp 220 is a starburst galaxy, packed with very new, hot, young stars. It probably formed when two spiral galaxies merged.*

The Hubble Deep Field

In December 1995, the *Hubble Space Telescope* was pointed at a single stretch of sky for ten consecutive days. It revealed no fewer than 1,500 galaxies at various stages of evolution. Some are four billion times fainter than can be seen by the naked eye, and date back to near the beginning of the Universe. This so-called Hubble Deep Field is beginning to give astronomers clues about how many galaxies there are in the Universe, and how they formed.

is is what the Hubble Space Telescope *saw when it took a ten-day*
re of a patch of sky close to the constellation of the Big Dipper.
lubble Deep Field is made up of 342 exposures and contains 1,500
es, some of them among the faintest and most distant ever seen.

Violent Galaxies

In 1963, Maartin Schmidt, an astronomer in California, was examining the spectrum of light from a faint blue, starlike object known as 3C 273. To his astonishment, he realized that, although it more than three billion light years away and moving away from Ea at almost 31,070 miles (50,000 km) per second, it was giving out int radiation. These distant objects became known as quasistellar radio sources, or quasars for short. They appear starlike because they emit a hundred times more energy than our entire galaxy, but from an area not much bigger than our Solar System. The *Hubble Space Telescope* has revealed that quasars are, in fact, blindingly bright objects embedded in the centers of distant galaxies.

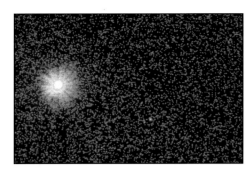

△ *The first quasar to be identified was 3C 273, viewed here in x rays. Although starlike in appearance, quasars are very distant and intensely active galaxies.*

Monster black holes

There is only one power source that could generate the immense energy of quasars—black holes. Most quasars are found in colliding galaxies. As the galaxies merge, gas and stars are stirred up and begin to spiral around a black hole that lies at the center of one, or even both galaxies. As matter is sucked in, an accretion disk is created, similar to those around black holes formed from dying stars in our own galaxy. But in the case of quasars, the black holes must be incredibly massive, each perhaps a billion times the mass of the Sun.

▽ *The galaxy M87, in the Virgo cluster, sends out a narrow jet of matter from its core. The activity in this galaxy is probably caused by a giant black hole.*

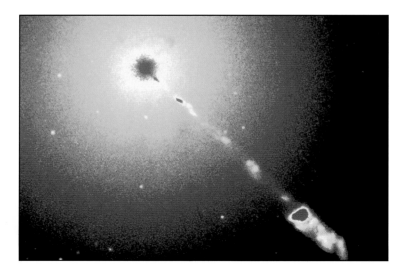

△ *A great cloud of swirling gas and star debris spirals down toward a black hole millions of times the mass of the Sun. At the same time, it gives out x rays and powerful jets of radio-emitting gas. Many of the violent processes taking place in the cores of galaxies are probably similar events seen from different angles.*

△ *In this computer simulation, two spiral galaxies have collided and passed one another. Spiral arms have been dragged out into a bridge of matter between them.*

Galactic activity

Not all galaxies fit into the neat classification of spiral, elliptical, irregular, or even quasar. Many are being torn apart by immense explosions. Others, like M87 in the Virgo cluster, have a single great jet of matter spiraling out from the core. It seems likely that all these different galaxies have a massive black hole at their center. In some cases, the black hole becomes active each time it is fed with gas and stars.

In other galaxies, the black hole remains dormant. There is good reason to believe that every galaxy, including our own, has a black hole at its center.

△ *The Cartwheel Galaxy is the result of a collision in which one galaxy passed straight through the middle of another spiral galaxy.*

◁ *Light bent by gravity creates the illusion of a cluster of five different quasars, when in fact there is only one. It is called Einstein's cross.*

Gravitational lens

When astronomers identified two identical quasars lying next to each other, they were puzzled. The explanation quickly dawned—it was something first predicted by Einstein, who realized that light is bent by a strong gravitational field. If there is a massive object such as a cluster of galaxies between us and the quasar, the light from the quasar becomes bent, as if through a lens. If the alignment is right, light will be bent through several routes to create a multiple image. This can take the form of a cross, for example, or even a clover leaf.

Echoes of Creation

The Universe is flying apart. Trace all the lines of the expanding galaxies back in time, and it appears they all originated from the same place. If so, they must have been blown apart by an incredible explosion. In the 1950s, the English astronomer Fred Hoyle and others suggested a different explanation. They argued that the Universe, though expanding, remains essentially the same, with new matter created to fill the expanding gaps. This is known as the Steady State Universe, and Fred Hoyle called the alternative the Big Bang Universe. The name stuck and some scientists predicted that we would find a way of proving that the Big Bang really happened. If the Universe did begin in an explosion, it would have left an echo. The incredible heat of the explosion would now have cooled to just a few degrees above absolute zero −460°F (−273°C), but even so it should be detectable.

◁ *The* Cosmic Background Explor[er] *satellite,* COBE, *was launched in 19[..] to study the microwave background radiation left over from the Big Ban[g] over 12 billion years ago. Scientists [are] now beginning to build up a very detailed map of the early Universe.*

▽ *You can listen to the sound of the Big Bang in your own home! If you tune your television between stations, the picture will "snow," and the sound will hiss. About one percent of this noise is from the microwave background, reaching us from the Big Bang itself.*

Whispers from space

When the first transatlantic communications satellite, *Telstar*, was launched in 1962, a big radio antenna was constructed in New Jersey [to] receive its signal. But the antenna also received a faint hiss that would[n't] go away, even when two astronomers, Robert Wilson and Arno Penzia[s,] removed pigeon droppings from the receiver! The hiss seemed to come from every direction and radiated energy at a temperature just 37 degr[ees] above absolute zero. They realized that this must be the background radiation left from the Big Bang itself. To date, this is the best eviden[ce] that the Universe really did begin in a fireball.

Cosmic ripples

In 1990, NASA launched *COBE*, the *Cosmic Background Explorer* satellite. Its purpose was to stare at the microwave background. The first result was a spectacular confirmation that the radiation is a perfect example of so-called "black body" radiation—radiation simply due to heat. *COBE* then started to map it and look for features. The radiation turned out to be very, very smooth in every direction. Eventually, patterns began to emerge and, in 1992, scientists announced that they had seen ripples in the background. This caused a sensation. The fluctuations are only thirty millionths of a degree, but they provided the early Universe with enough variation in density for the very first stars and galaxies to be born. Without them, the Universe would still be a diffuse haze of gas.

▽ *Robert Wilson and Arno Penzias stand in front of the radio antenna with which they discovered the microwave background radiation in 1962. The antenna was originally designed to pick up signals from the communications satellite, Telstar.*

map of the cosmic background radiation is
rue map, since some of the signal was due
mth in COBE's instruments. Even so, it
ned that the present structure of the
se originated in the Big Bang. When the
ery was made, the leader of the project
ed it as "like seeing the face of God."

. light

ireball of the Big Bang gave off no light. Light could not travel in
ht lines without bumping into things—atoms had not yet formed
he Universe was a seething mass of particles. After about 300,000
, the Universe had cooled enough for atoms to form. The Universe
ne transparent and radiation could shine freely. The microwave
ground radiation is the cooled remnant of that first light.

e discovery of the background radiation sent out ripples
h astronomy. The theory of the Steady State Universe
h rejects the Big Bang theory) was finally discredited.

The Big Bang

Astronomers can trace the expanding Universe back to a time when all the stars and galaxies they can see must have been squashed together into a tiny space. They can look back directly to the cosmic background radiation emitted when our Universe was about 300,000 years old and only slightly larger than our own galaxy. To journey back farther, toward the Big Bang itself, it is necessary to turn to physics. Scientists have studied conditions back to within a hundredth of a billionth of a second of the start of the Universe by recreating them in high-energy particle colliders. And their theories take them even further.

A note on scale

The numbers in cosmology are so vast the numbers in subatomic physics are tiny that scientists use a special shorth Ten multiplied by itself (i.e., a hundre written as 10^2. A thousand is 10^3. Simi a tenth is 10^{-1}, a thousandth 10^{-3}, and s

△ *Einstein's famous equation $E=mc^2$ shows that it takes a lot of energy to make a little matter. In the first instant of the Big Bang (1), all four fundamental forces of nature act as one, and even space and time are unified.*

△ *By 10^{-32} seconds (2), the Universe is a hot, seething mass of particles, expanding at the speed of light. At 10^{-11} seconds (3), the weak nuclear force separates from electromagnetism. Quarks and antiquarks are spontaneously created and annihilate each other.*

In the beginning

The entire Universe may have been born from a single subatomic particle! Today, every speck of seemingly empty space is a seething well of potential energy. Physicists suspect that a whole range of particles are being born from it every instant. Usually, they die again before they have had time to do anything, go anywhere, or be seen by anyone. But, just occasionally, they can get trapped and become "real." No one really knows for sure, but this is possibly how the Universe came into being.

Superforce

There are just four fundamental forces at work in the Universe—gravity, the strong and weak nuclear force and electromagnetism. But they may all have been u into a single superforce that governed the Universe at moment of its birth. As the Universe cooled, each of forces separated. Gravity was the first to separate, at j 10^{-43} seconds after the start. The strong force followed 10^{-35} seconds; the weak force and electromagnetism went their separate ways at 10^{-11} seconds.

r 300,000 years (6), radiation is no longer
enough to break up atoms. The Universe
s transparent and light shines through it.
ne billion years (7), clumps of gas are
together to form protogalaxies. Inside
he first stars are beginning to shine.

7

$\triangledown$ Today (8), after 12 billion years, clusters of
galaxies have formed superclusters. Matter
has been processed through several
generations of stars to form the
building materials for
planets and life.

8

0^4 seconds (4), the Universe is about the
the Solar System, and the temperature
len enough for quarks to form protons,
ns, and other so-called baryons. After
onds (5), protons and neutrons link up.

$\triangle$ The background
image shows the tracks of
subatomic particles. Scientists create these
high-energy collisions to explore conditions
similar to those after the Big Bang.

ion

ess called inflation might explain how something
er than an atom grew to a universe the size of a
fruit in the first 10^{-32} of a second. If a little bubble
Universe continued expanding after the strong
r force should have separated from it, it might have
d a false vacuum, a kind of antigravity. This would
the bubble to expand 100 times faster than the
of light. When inflation froze, it released so much
y that it produced all the matter in our Universe.

First atom

When the strong force separated, the Universe heated
up to 10^{27} degrees. Matter and antimatter were created
in equal proportions. An imbalance in the process led
to a build-up of matter, which is why there are no
antigalaxies today. The first particles were quarks and
electrons. As the Universe cooled, quarks combined to
form protons and neutrons. Some of them clustered
together to make helium nuclei and, after 300,000 years,
the electrons joined them to make the first atoms.

▽ *If gravity wins, the Universe is heading*
the Big Crunch. At first it contracts slowl
faster and faster. Galaxies are pus
closer and closer together b
merging and feedin
giant black l

2

◁ *The x-ray*
glow from this cloud (
be evidence of the dark matt
makes up most of the Universe's m

◁ *The object to the right of this star (2) is a*
dwarf, a star too small to become a nuclear f
Brown dwarfs may add up to more mass tha

The Great Unknown

There are some questions about the nature of the Universe that, until recently, seemed to be unanswerable. What [ma]kes up the Universe? How heavy is it? How old is it, and how [will] it all end? Astronomers still do not have all the answers, [but] at last they feel able to begin researching the questions. [To d]o so will take some very strange telescopes. As well as [takin]g the best measurements possible from optical, infrared, [and] radio telescopes on the ground and in space, astronomers [who] also are using instruments deep underground to try to weigh the Universe and predict its ultimate fate.

△ *The Universe could end in three ways: The closed or Big Crunch Universe (1) is so massive it collapses under its own weight. In the flat Universe (2), expansion slows down, but never quite leads to collapse. The open Universe (3) expands forever.*

◁ *As the Universe approaches its end, the remaining matter spirals into black holes. Nothing can hold the Universe back from the final inferno. But perhaps it could bounce back in a new Big Bang.*

Dark matter

All that we can see is only a fraction of the Universe. Some matter is detectable only by its gravitational [ef]fects on the rotation of galaxies. This is called [dark] matter, and no one knows its material composition. [This] matter could be conventional matter, such as [faint] stars called brown dwarfs, or even black holes.

[Gho]stly particles

[Dark] matter may also include neutrinos—ghostly [partic]les once thought to have no mass. These are so [nume]rous that any mass at all would make them far [heavi]er than all the stars. Other particles are predicted [by ph]ysicists, but have yet to be detected. If found, [they c]ould make up 99 percent of the Universe.

The fate of the Universe

From its birth, now thought to be between 12 and 15 billion years ago, the Universe has continued to expand. It would take a hundred times more mass than is contained in the visible Universe to halt this expansion completely. If this happened, the Universe would contract into the Big Crunch. This could be the end of everything, or the start of a new Universe.

Heat death

Other evidence suggests that the Universe is not sufficiently dense to halt the expansion. Stars will slowly age and die. Galaxies will fade away and even black holes will disappear. After billions and billions of years, the Universe will become a cold, dull place, containing only a few widely spaced particles.

△ *Alice*
enters a wormhole
in space-time. It could take her
to another time, or even into
another universe.

△ *Space itself can be curved, so a*
wormhole might act as a shortcut
between two seemingly distant pl...

Beyond Time

Time is relative. The rate your watch ticks relative to someone else's depends on how fast you are moving relative to each other. This was Alb... Einstein's conclusion in 1905. He established that, as the speed of light must the same for everyone, no matter how they are moving, then space and time themselves must be intertwined. Einstein developed these ideas in his general theory of relativity, taking gravity into account and showing how gravity ben... space-time. Many science-fiction writers and some scientists have seized on Einstein's theories to show that one day time travel may just be possible.

△ *Time appears to run in*
one direction only. Broken
eggs do not reassemble
themselves. This tendency
to disorder is one of the
few natural arrows in time.

Time's arrow

We all have a strong sense of passing time, and time always seems to run in one direction only. For example, people age, and cups of coffee cool off. However, according to the laws of physics, there is nothing to prevent most processes from reversing. In fact, in many processes, especially at the level of particles, there is no distinguishable arrow of time.

Warping space and time

The Universe's fundamental speed limit seems to be the speed of light—190,000 (300,000 km) per second. Even though a spaceship never could travel this fast, it m... in theory, be possible to warp the space ar... it, shrinking space ahead and expanding behind. The snag is that distorting space this way would require at least a million times the energy locked up in the Sun!

...eedledum and
...ledee are identical
... Tweedledum sets
... a round trip to a
... star, at almost
...ed of light. The
...y seems to him to
...aken only a few
... When he returns,
...ds that time has
... more quickly for
...ledee, who is now
... years older.

...rmholes

...ossibility for time travel, in theory at least, is a
...nhole—a cosmic tunnel built from exotic matter
...een different regions of space-time. Just as in
...ck hole, time in a wormhole slows to a standstill
...he laws of our Universe break down. But if one
... be kept open long enough, it might be possible
...erge from a wormhole unharmed.

...e paradoxes

... travel raises many paradoxes. For example,
...u could travel back in time, you would have
...hance to kill your own grandfather before
...father was born. That would mean you also
... never born, so how could you begin your
...ey? Either reverse time travel should be
...dden or there would be an infinite number
...iverses, one for every possibility. Maybe it
...re simple to stick to the here and now!

*...en Alice steps through the wormhole, she
...rs instantaneously in another part of the Universe.*

The Search for E.T.

Are people on the Earth alone in the Universe? As yet, there is no certain evidence of life anywhere else, much less intelligent life. But there are hundreds of millions of stars in our galaxy. If a fraction have habitable planets and a fraction of those developed life, there could be millions of civilizations other than our own. However, the distances between the stars is so great it is unlikely that extraterrestrials—if they exist—have visited our planet. We do not even know exactly how life began on the Earth. The evidence we do have, however, suggests that it takes several billion years of evolution for intelligent life to arise and to develop the technology capable of sending messages to the stars.

△ *The plaque fixed to* Voyager 1 *describes where it comes from and who built it. It also carries a record of natural sounds of the Earth as well as music.*

The search for distant planets

Our best telescopes could never see a distant planet against the glare of its star. But big planets make stars wobble as they orbit, and several wobbling stars have been detected. Most of these stars wobble due to Jupiterlike planets that are inhospitable to humans, but some planets may be far enough away from their stars to be hospitable. Far out in space, telescopes in the future may see distant planets directly. They may even be able to detect gases, such as ozone and water vapor, that may indicate life.

△ *In 1974, the first signal to possibl alien life was broadcast from the wo biggest radio dish at Arecibo in Pue Rico. Arecibo has remained the cent for the search to identify alien signa*

The search for extraterrestrial intelligence

Since the first radio broadcast, radio signals have been traveling out beyond our planet at the speed of light. Th signals have already passed many stars and planets, but unless aliens were listening for them, they would not no The most powerful radio signal to have left the Earth w sent from a radio telescope at Arecibo, Puerto Rico in 19 It was a brief digital signal describing who and where w and it was directed at a cluster of stars known as M13. E at the speed of light, however, it will take 25,000 years t reach its destination. Many teams are taking part in SET (the Search for Extra-Terrestrial Intelligence). They sca Sunlike star systems with radio telescopes, analyzing mi of radio frequencies by computer in the search for a sigr

△ *A scientist discharges an electric field across a mixture of water, hydrogen, methane, and ammonia. In this experiment, amino acids—the basis of life on this planet—accumulate after a time, just as they may once have done on the early Earth.*

... look like these mounds
... Similar structures may have
... the first inhabitants of the
... than 3.5 billion years ago.

△ *Alien existence is a subject
clouded by fiction and fraud.
The "flying saucer" above
proved to be a child's toy
photographed at close range.
Though many people claim to
have been visited or abducted
by aliens, there is still no
evidence of the presence of
other beings in the Universe.*

life on other planets

... ere are aliens out there, what are they like?
... n the Earth shows great variety and ingenuity and it
... bable that life on another planet would do the same.
... ght be based on a different chemistry entirely, with
... or silicon taking the place of carbon, or with the role
... ter being played by liquid ammonia. Physically, life
... will need to do some of the same things as humans.
... may need to move around, sense their environment,
... nd defend themselves. They would probably have a
... and a back, but eyes, hands, and so on could all be
... ed by other tools, and not necessarily in pairs.

△ *This bright light was photographed over
São Paulo, Brazil in 1984. It is one of many
so-called UFOs—Unidentified Flying Objects.*

Impossible Questions

Throughout this book, we have seen how astronomers obser our planet, our Solar System, our Galaxy, and some of the billions of other galaxies beyond it. One day, in theory, we coul learn every detail of the physical Universe. But there are still s questions that can never be answered with certainty. For examp what lies beyond or before our Universe? Why did the Universe be Why are we here in it? By showing us that the Earth is not the center of the Universe, astronomy has led us to question our own importance in the grand scheme of life. But some of the answers to these big questions could put us at center stage again.

△ *Every culture has proposed a supreme being as the creator of the Universe. Scientists can offer few better explanations for the fundamental laws of the cosmos.*

Beyond the horizon

The farthest galaxies seem to be receding from us so fast that they are approaching the speed of light. We cannot see beyond them. The Universe may be infinite, or it may end just beyond this light horizon. We cannot tell. Perhaps our Universe is just one bubble in a whole foam of universes. Some may not have inflated, while others might have different physical laws or dimensions from our own Universe.

The living Universe

Perhaps, when a black hole forms in our Universe, it gives birth to another universe somewhere else. If the new universe can inherit the ability to make black holes, then universes might evolve and get better and better at making black holes. A universe like our own, which is good at creating black holes, is also good at making stars and ultimately planets and life itself.

▷ *Black holes may give birth to new universes. The colored peaks in this computer simulation are other universes, each with its own physical laws.*

e same force that makes apples fall also
stars together. The same force that makes
radioactive blows the elements out from
ding stars to form new stars and planets.
ame force that gives us electricity also
the Universe transparent. It is as if the
rse has been designed for us to study it.

Cosmic coincidences

Life may seem like a lottery, the Universe like a random accident. Perhaps the biggest coincidence of all is that our Universe is just right for life. If, for example, beryllium nuclei, made in the cores of stars, were a different size, they would not go on to form carbon and oxygen, elements essential for life. If the weak nuclear force were slightly different, stars would not explode as supernovae, spewing their elements out to form potential new stars and planets. But if the force of gravity were slightly stronger, all stars would collapse into black holes. The list goes on, raising the question of whether our Universe is meant to be the way it is.

The ultimate question

The final question is: Why we are here? Cosmologists point out how the Universe is finely tuned for complexity and life. This is called the "weak anthropic principle." More controversially, it has also been suggested that this is more than coincidence, and that the Universe *must* produce intelligent observers. Some even argue that observers are necessary to bring the Universe into being, and that ultimately everything that exists must be known. If that is true, astronomy has a bright future and we are back at the center of the Universe.

▽ *On a small, blue planet, the third rock*
from an average star in a typical spiral
galaxy, a life form developed with the
potential to understand the Universe. Why?

Universal Facts

THE PLANETS OF THE SOLAR SYSTEM

NAME	DISTANCE FROM SUN (Miles)	DIAMETER (Miles)	MASS (Earth=1)	ROTATION	YEAR	MOONS
Mercury	35,980,000	3,031	0.055	58.66 days	87.97 days	0
Venus	67,230,000	7,521	0.81	243.01 days	224.7 days	0
Earth	93,000,000	8,000	1.00	23.93 hrs	365.26 days	1
Mars	141,600,000	4,223	0.11	24.62 hrs	686.98 days	2
Jupiter	483,600,000	88,846	318	9.92 hrs	11.86 years	16
Saturn	888,200,000	74,898	95.18	10.67 hrs	29.46 years	23
Uranus	1,786,400,000	31,763	14.50	17.23 hrs	84.01 years	15
Neptune	2,798,800,000	30,800	17.14	16.12 hrs	164.79 years	8
Pluto	3,666,200,000	1,430	0.0022	6.375 days	248.54 years	1

BRIGHTEST STARS (in order of apparent brightness)

NAME	TYPE	LOCATION	DISTANCE (Light years)	APPARENT MAGNITUDE	ABSOLUTE MAGNITUDE
Sirius	White Major	Canis	8.6	-1.46	1.4
Canopus	Yellow Giant	Carina	1200	-0.72	-8.5
Alpha Centauri	Yellow	Centaurus	4.3	-0.27	4
Arcturus	Orange Giant	Botes	36	-0.04	-0.2
Vega	White	Lyra	25	0.03	0.5
Capella	Yellow	Auriga	43	0.08	-0.7
Rigel	Blue Giant	Orion	900	0.12	-7.1
Procyon	Yellow Minor	Canis	11	0.38	2.6
Achernar	Blue Giant	Erudanus	85	0.46	-1.6
Betelgeux	Red Giant	Orion	310	0.5	5.6
Agena	Blue Giant	Centaurus	460	0.61	-5.1
Altair	White	Aquila	17	0.77	2.2
Acrux	Binary	Southern Cross	360	0.83	-3.9
Aldebaran	Orange	Taurus	68	0.85	-0.3
Antares	Red Giant	Scorpius	330	0.96	-4.7
Spica	Blue Giant	Virgo	260	0.98	-3.6
Pollux	Orange Giant	Gemini	36	1.14	0.2
Fomalhaut	White	Piscis Australis	22	1.16	2.0
Deneb	White Giant	Cygnus	1800	1.25	-7.5
Beta Crucis	Blue Giant	Southern Cross	425	1.25	-5.0
Regulus	Blue	Leo	85	1.35	-0.6

FIRSTS IN ASTRONOMY

1600 B.C.	Babylonian star catalogs compiled
270 B.C.	Aristarchos proposes that the Earth revolves around the Su
230 B.C.	Eratosthenes measures the Earth's circumference
135 B.C.	Hipparchos discovers that the Earth's axis wobbles
A.D. 127	Ptolemy develops the Earth-centered theory of the Unive
1054	Chinese observe the Crab supernova
1543	Copernicus revives the idea of a Sun-centered Universe
1609	Kepler describes the orbits of planets
1609	Galileo is first to use a telesc for astronomy
1655	Huygens discovers Saturn's r
1668	Newton makes first reflectir telescope
1687	Newton publishes Theory of Gravitation
1705	Halley recognizes that come orbit the Sun
1781	Herschel discovers Uranus
1838	Bessel measures the distance of a star
1846	Adams and Leverrier predic existence of Neptune
1912	Leavitt discovers Cepheid variable stars
1920	Slipher discovers that nebul are receding
1923	Hubble shows that receding nebulae are galaxies
1938	Bethe and Weizsäcker sugge stars are powered by nuclea fusion
1963	Schmidt discovers the first quasar
1965	Penzias and Wilson discover microwave background radi
1967	Jocelyn Bell discovers first pu
1992	COBE satellite identifies rip in the microwave backgroun

Note: The lower the value of the magnitude, the brighter the star.

Apparent magnitude is how bright the star seems from the Earth.

Absolute magnitude is how bright it would seem if all the stars were the same distance from the Earth.

..JOR TELESCOPES—Optical/infrared

E	LOCATION	DIAMETER (feet)	FIRST LIGHT
	Chile	52 ft. equivalent	1998
	Hawaii	6 x 32	1990
..Hopkins	Arizona	21.3	1998
..nchukskaya	Russia	19.6	1976
	California	16.4	1948
..chel	Canary Islands	13.7	1987
..o Tololo	Chile	13	1976
..all	Arizona	12.4	1973
..o-Australian	Australia	12.7	1975
..InfraRed	Hawaii	12.4	1978
..ble	Space	7.8	1990

..JOR PLANETARY PROBES

E	NATION	LAUNCH	TARGET	RESULT
..ner 2	U.S.A.	1962	Venus	First flyby
..ra 3	U.S.S.R.	1965	Venus	Crushed during descent
..ner 4, 6, & 7	U.S.A.	1964, '69, '69	Mars	Flybys
..ra 7	U.S.S.R.	1970	Venus	Landed. Survived 23 minutes
..s 2 & 3	U.S.S.R.	1971	Mars	2: Orbiter, dropped flag 3: Orbiter and lander
..ner 9	U.S.A.	1971	Mars	Orbiter
..er 10	U.S.A.	1972	Jupiter	Flyby 1973
..er 11	U.S.A.	1973	Jupiter and Saturn	Jupiter flyby 1974 Saturn flyby 1979
..g 1 & 2	U.S.A.	1975	Mars	Orbiters and landers
..ger 1	U.S.A.	1977	Jupiter and Saturn	Jupiter flyby 1979 Saturn flyby 1980
..ger 2	U.S.A.	1977	Grand Tour	Flybys: Jupiter 1979, Saturn 1981, Uranus 1986, Neptune 1989
..er Venus	U.S.A.	1978	Venus	Orbiter
..ra 13	U.S.S.R.	1981	Venus	Landed, lasted 2 hours
..ra 15	U.S.S.R.	1983	Venus	Radar mapper
..1	U.S.S.R.	1984	Venus	Lander and balloon, plus Halley's Comet flyby
..ellan	U.S.A.	1989	Venus	Radar mapper
..eo	U.S.A.	1989	Jupiter	Orbiter plus probe. Arrived 1995
..finder	U.S.A.	1996	Mars	Lander and rover
..al Surveyor	U.S.A.	1996	Mars	Mapping orbiter
..ni	U.S.A./ Europe	1997	Saturn	Orbiter and Titan probe

FIRSTS IN SPACE
1957	*Sputnik 1* (U.S.S.R.) first satellite launched
1958	*Explorer 1* (U.S.A.) discovers Van Allen radiation belts
1959	*Luna 1* (U.S.S.R.) escapes Earth's gravity
1959	*Vanguard 2* (U.S.A.) takes first photos of the Earth
1959	*Luna 2* (U.S.S.R.) hits the Moon
1959	*Luna 3* (U.S.S.R.) returns first pictures of far side of the Moon
1960	*TIROS 1* (U.S.A.) first weather satellite
1960	*ECHO 1* (U.S.A.) first communications satellite
1961	*Vostok 1* (U.S.S.R.) first manned orbital flight
1962	*Aerobee* (U.S.A.) x-ray satellite launched
1963	*Vostok 6* (U.S.S.R.) carries first woman in orbit
1965	*Early Bird* (U.S.A.) commercial geostationary communications satellite
1965	*Gemini 6* (U.S.A.) manned rendezvous in space
1966	*Luna 9* (U.S.S.R.) soft Moon landing
1969	*Apollo 11* (U.S.A.) manned lunar landing
1975	Apollo/Soyuz first international linkup
1978	Launch of *International Ultraviolet Explorer* (U.S.A./Europe)
1981	*Columbia* (U.S.A.) first space shuttle flight
1986	Launch of *Mir* space station
1990	*Hubble Space Telescope* (U.S.A./Europe) launched
1998	Launch of first component of *International Space Station*

Glossary

Accretion disk A disk of matter that builds up around a dense object as material spirals down toward it. It is believed that accretion disks often form around black holes.

Antimatter A form of matter, such as an opposite electrical charge, that shares properties with the fundamental particles of matter, but in reverse.

Asteroid A rocky or metallic minor planet orbiting the Sun. Most asteroids lie between the orbits of Mars and Jupiter in the asteroid belt.

Astronomical unit The average distance between the Earth and the Sun (927,506 miles). It is a useful unit for expressing distances in the Solar System.

Atmosphere A layer of gas surrounding a planet, star, or moon.

Billion One thousand million (1,000,000,000).

Binary star A pair of stars in orbit around the common center of gravity between them (i.e., around each other).

Black hole A region of space-time where there is such a concentration of matter, and consequently gravity, that not even light can escape. Black holes can form when massive stars collapse. Others lie at the heart of active galaxies.

Brown dwarf A small star of such low mass (less than 8 percent of the Sun's mass) that nuclear fusion reactions cannot begin. A brown dwarf shines only because of the faint heat released as it contracts.

Cepheid variable A class of star that varies its brightness in a regular period of between one and fifty days.

Cluster A group of stars or galaxies affecting each other by their gravitational attraction, or force.

Comet An object made of ice, dust, and other material. There may be billions of comets beyond the orbit of Pluto. Some come nearer the Sun, on elliptical orbits, leaving spectacular tails of gas and dust.

Constellation A grouping of stars in the same direction in the sky, though not necessarily associated with each other.

Corona The outer atmosphere of the Sun, extending many millions of miles above the visible surface. The corona can reach 3,600,032°F and is visible during eclipses.

Cosmic background radiation Microwave radiation coming from all directions in the sky and thought to be the cooled remnant of the fireball of the Big Bang in which the Universe began.

Cosmology The study of the structure and origin of the Universe.

Crater Circular depression on a planet, moon, or asteroid, usually resulting from the impact of another body.

Dark matter Matter known to exist, but mostly invisible. It might be normal matter in the form of brown dwarfs or black holes, or it could be ghostly, unidentified particles.

Eclipse A shadow cast by one celestial object on another. For example, the Earth's shadow falling on the Moon causes a lunar eclipse. The Moon's shadow falling on the Earth is seen as a solar eclipse.

Escape velocity The velocity that a projectile must reach if it is to escape from the gravity of an astronomical object without further propulsion.

Event horizon The boundary of a black hole, beyond which neither matter nor radiation can escape from within it.

False-color Color added by computer to enhance the details of an image.

Galaxy A celestial city of millions or billions of stars, gas, and dust bound together by their gravitational pull.

Gamma rays The most energetic radiation in the electromagnetic spectrum.

Globular cluster A spherical cluster of between a few thousand and a million stars. Globular clusters form the halo of our galaxy and contain very ancient stars.

Gravitational lens A region of mass, such as a cluster of galaxies, which bends light from more distant objects.

Gravity An attractive force between matter, related to mass. Although weak, gravity acts over large distances.

Hubble constant The rate at which the Universe is expanding. As the galaxies move farther apart, this causes redshift, which can be used to measure the rate of expansion.

Infrared radiation Electromagnetic radiation of a longer wavelength than light but less than radio.

Light year The distance that light travels in one year (5,865,634 miles).

Local Group The group of about 30 galaxies in which our own galaxy is found.

Magnetosphere The magnetic bubble around the Earth or another planet in which ionized gas is contained by the planet's magnetic field.

Main sequence The range of temperature and brightness which the majority of stars spend most of their lives.

r A brilliant streak
the sky caused by
, such as specks of dust
s, burning up as they
he Earth's atmosphere.
rs are popularly known
oting stars.

rite A lump of rock or
that has fallen to the
from space. The largest
rites create craters on
t.

a A cloud of gas or
space.

ino A particle with no
and little or no mass.

on star A star that
en so compressed that
ns and protons have
quashed together to
neutrons. It has the
f a star but is much
r.

Cloud A cloud of
ns or even billions of
nt comets thought to
yond the orbit of Pluto.

The path of one body
d another, such as the
around the Earth or
rth around the Sun.
y be circular, or more
elliptical.

lax The apparent
n of an object against
e distant background
d by a changing
oint. It provides a
or calculating the
ces to nearby stars.

Perihelion The closest point
to the Sun in the orbit of a
body such as a comet or planet.

Photon The smallest particle
of energy that can be carried
as light.

Planet A body in orbit
around the Sun or another star,
shining in reflected light only.
Bodies over 620 miles across
are normally considered to
be planets. Smaller objects
are called minor planets.

Planetary nebula A cloud
of gas that can look like a
planet, but really consists
of expanding shells of gas
thrown off by a star close
to the end of its life.

Protostar An early stage in
the formation of a star before
nuclear fusion has begun.

Pulsar A spinning neutron star
emitting bursts of radiation,
like a flashing lighthouse beam,
often many times a second.

Quasar The energetic core of
an active galaxy. Quasars give
out as much energy as a big
galaxy from a region no bigger
than our Solar System. Quasar
is short for quasistellar object.

Red dwarf A small, dim, red
star with a temperature of
less than 9,032°F.

Red giant A bright red star
up to 100 times the diameter
of the Sun and thought to be
near the end of its life.

Redshift The stretching of
light from an object, such as a
galaxy, that is moving away
from us. Because the Universe
is still expanding, the higher
the redshift, the more distant
the object.

Satellite Any object in orbit
around another object. The
term is normally applied to a
moon or an artificial craft
orbiting around a planet.

Solar wind The stream of
electrically charged particles
blowing from the Sun. When
it strikes molecules of air in
the Earth's atmosphere, it
produces the curtain of light
known as the aurora.

Space-time The combination
of the three dimensions of
space plus one of time.
Space-time makes up the
fabric of the Universe.

Spectrum The rainbow band
of electromagnetic radiation
of different wavelengths. The
light from a star or galaxy,
split up into its wavelengths
of different colors.

Subatomic physics The
study of the fundamental
particles that make up
atoms, and the forces that
act between them.

Sunspot A dark spot on the
surface, or photosphere, of the
Sun, caused by a magnetic
disturbance. A sunspot is
slightly cooler than the
surrounding area.

Supercluster A grouping
made up of clusters of galaxies.
Superclusters can be hundreds
of millions of light years across.

Supernova An exploding,
massive star torn apart by an
intense flash of radiation.
This happens when the core
of a star collapses.

Ultraviolet radiation
Electromagnetic radiation
of shorter wavelength than
the blue end of the visible
spectrum.

Universe Space-time and
everything contained within
it. In theory, there might be
universes other than our own,
but we could not have direct
knowledge of them, or they
would be part of our own
Universe.

Van Allen belts The belts of
radiation around the Earth
caused by charged particles
trapped in the Earth's
magnetic field.

Wavelength The distance
between successive peaks (or
troughs) in a wave, such as
electromagnetic radiation.

White dwarf A hot, compact
star no heavier than 1.4 times
the mass of the Sun. With
most of its nuclear fuel used
up, the star contracts until it
is very dense and hot.

X rays Electromagnetic
radiation of shorter wavelength
than ultraviolet radiation.

Index

Acknowledgments

The publishers would like to thank the following illustrators for their contribution to this book:

Julian Baum 6–7, 10–11 (*background*), 24–25, 26–27, 29*cr* & *br*, 30*tl* & *bl*, 31*tr*, 32–33, 34–35, 36*tl*, 37*br*, 38–39, 40–41, 42–43, 44–45, 46–47, 48–49, 50–51, 52–53, 54–55, 56*tl*, 57*tr*, 58–59, 60–61, 65*br*, 66*bl*, 68–69, 72–73, 76–77; **Jim Burns** 12–13, 14–15; **Tom Connell** 13*br*, 14*tl*, 15*br*, 16*b*, 17*tl*; **Bernard Gudynas/ZAP ART** Icons, 20–21, 66–67, 70–71, 84–85, 88–89;

Peter Gudynas/ZAP ART 22–23, 78–79, 80–81 82–83, 86–87; **Ceri Llewellyn** 9*bl*, 37*cl*, 56*br*, 59*cl*, 62*tl*.

The publishers would also like to thank the following: Clarissa Claudel, Peter Clayman, Sarah Goodwin, Ian Graham, Justin Hobson at the Science Photo Library, Charlotte Hurdman, Pauline Newman, Robin Redfern, Camilla Reid, Miranda Smith, Julie Tatnell, Marc Wilson.

The publishers would like to thank the following for supplying photographs:

Page 6 Zefa *tl*, Science Photo Library *tr*, Bridgeman Art Library *c*; 7 Science Photo Library *t*, Corbis U.K. *c*; 8 Scala *tl*, Carnegie Institute of Washington *bl*, Mary Evans Picture Library *cr*, Getty Images *background image*; 9 Science Photo Library *tl*, Galaxy Picture Library *tr*, Frank Spooner Pictures *br*; 10 Planet Earth Pictures *tr*, NASA *cr*, ESA *bl*; 11 NASA *tr*, ESA *cr*, *bc*; 12 Planet Earth Pictures *l*, E.T. Archive *tc*, Popperfoto *tr*, Corbis U.K. *c*; 13 Novosti *tl*, Science Photo Library *tc*, Frank Spooner Pictures *cr*; 14 NASA *bl*, Frank Spooner Pictures *bc*; 13 Genesis Space Picture Library *c*; 16 Frank Spooner Pictures *tl*, Telegraph Colour Library *bl*; 16/17 Frank Spooner Pictures; 17 Science Photo Library *bl*, *br*, ESA *c*; 18 Science Photo Library *tl*, *bc*, NASA *b*, Novosti *cr*; 18/19 NASA *c*; 19 NASA/Portfolio Pictures *tr*; Science Photo Library *cl*, *bl*, Galaxy Picture Library *cr*; 20 Galaxy Picture Library *bl*, Popperfoto *bc*, Telstar *tr*, ESA/Meteosat *tc*; 21 NASA/ Mir/Hubble/ERS *t*, ESA/Exosat *bl*, Landsat 4/Planet Earth Pictures *c*, Getty Images *br*; 22 Meteosat/ESA *tl*, Planet Earth Pictures *tc*, Science Photo Library *cr*, *bl*; 23 NASA *tc*, Science Photo Library *bc*, Frank Spooner Pictures *br*; 26 Science Photo Library *tl*, Galaxy Picture Library *cl*; 27 Science Photo Library *t*; 28/29 Science Photo Library; 30 Science Photo Library *cl*; 30/31 Science Photo Library *c*, Bruce Coleman *b*; 31 ESA *bc*, Robert Harding Associates *br*; 32 Science Photo Library *tl*, Planet Earth Pictures *tr*, *bc*;

32/33 Science Photo Library *c*; 33 NASA *background image*; 34 Science Photo Library *tl*, *bl*; 35 Science Photo Library *cl*, *c*, *cr*, Planet Earth Pictures *cr*, Galaxy Picture Library *tc*, NASA *tr*, Planet Earth Pictures *br*, *background image*; 36 Science Photo Library *bl*; 37 Planet Earth Pictures *tl*, Ronald Grant *background image*, Science Photo Library *tr*, Galaxy Picture Library *c*; 38 Science Photo Library; 39 Zefa/Stockmarket *tc*; National Air Photo Library of Canada *tr*, Natural History Museum, London *bl*, *b*, Galaxy Picture Library *cl*; 40 Science Photo Library *cl*, *br*, NASA/Jet Propulsion Laboratory/U.S.A.; 41 NASA/Jet Propulsion Laboratory *tl*, *cr*, Planet Earth Pictures *tr*, Galaxy Picture Library *b*; 42 Planet Earth Pictures *bl*, *tr*; 41 Planet Earth Pictures *tl*, Galaxy Picture Library *cr*, *br*; 44 Planet Earth Pictures *tl*, Galaxy Picture Library *bl*, Science Photo Library *cr*, *bl*; 45 Science Photo Library *tl*, NASA/Jet Propulsion Laboratory *br*; 48 Science Photo Library bl, Galaxy Picture Library *br*; 49 Galaxy Picture Library *tc*, *tr*, *cr*, Telegraph Colour Library *bl*; 50/51 Galaxy Picture Library; 52 Science Photo Library *tl*, Galaxy Picture Library *cl*; 53 Galaxy Picture Library *tl*, Planet Earth Pictures *bl*; 54 Ann Ronan @ Image Select *tl*, Science Photo Library *cl*, *br*, Galaxy Picture Library *bl*; 55 E.T. Archive *tl*, Science Photo Library *bl*; 56/57 Science Photo Library; 58 Telegraph Colour Library *bl*, Science Photo Library br; 59 Martin Redfern *tl*, Science Photo Library *tr*; 60 Galaxy Picture Library *bl*, Martin Redfern/NASA/S. Stolovy, University of Arizona *br*; 61 Martin Redfern/ HST / NASA

Jeff Hester & Paul Scowen, Arizona State University *cl*, Martin Redfern/ NASA/ O'Dell *br*; 62 Galaxy Picture Library *bl*, Science Photo Library *cr*; 63 Science Photo Library *cl*, Martin Redfern *br*; 64 Science Photo Library *tl*, *bl*, Royal Observatory, Edinburgh *background image*, NASA/P. Garnavich, Harvard-Smithsonian Center Astrophysics *cr*; 64/65 Martin Redfern, Science Photo Library *bl*, *tr*; 66/67 original illustrations by John Tenniel from *Alice Adventures In Wonderland* by Lewis Carroll, 68 Science Photo Library; 69 Planet Earth Pictures *tr*, Science Photo Library *cl*, *cr*, Martin Redfern *br*; 70 Science Photo Library; 71 Galaxy Picture Library *t*, Neils Bohr Library/U.S.A. *b*; 78 Science Photo Library, 78/79 Planet Earth Pictures; 79 Science Photo Library *b*; 80/81 Science Photo Library *background image*; 82 Science Photo Library *bl*; 84 original illustrations by John Tenniel from *Through the Looking Glass* by Lewis Carroll; 86 NASA/Jet Propulsion Laboratory *tl*, Science Photo Library *bl*, Planet Earth Pictures *cr*; 86/87 Science Photo Library; 87 Fortean Picture Library *br*; 88 *The Ancient of Days* by William Blake *tl*; 89 International *bl*; **Endpapers** Getty Images.